Monster Movies

D1610917

Monster Movies

Emma Westwood

www.pocketessentials.com

First published in 2008 by Pocket Essentials

P.O. Box 394, Harpenden, Herts, AL5 1XJ

www.pocketessentials.com

A CIP catalogue record for this book is available from the British Library.

ISBN 978-1-84243-251-8

2 4 6 8 10 9 7 5 3 1

Typeset by Avocet Typeset, Chilton, Aylesbury, Bucks

Printed and bound in Great Britain by CPI Cox & Wyman, Reading, RG1 8EX

*Some People who Deserve
a Tickle on the Belly...*

Acknowledgements

(in non-discriminatory alphabetical order)

Mark Angeli, Kali Bateman, John Carpenter, Larry Cohen, Lisa Comerford, Bong Joon-ho, Cineclick Asia, Roger Corman, Guy Davis, Henry Ekselman, Keryn Ekselman, Nick Feik, Louise Heseltine, Christine Holder, Asha Holmes, Anne Hudson, Louise Jones, Ryuhei Kitamura, Adam Krentzman, Nicole Mazzocato, Greg McLean, Jean Meade, Ross Meade, Melbourne International Film Festival, Richard Moore, Ina Park, Hannah Patterson, Danielle Poulos, Cheryl Robinson, Kate Russell, Stephen Scoglio, Garry Seven, Adam Simon, Judy Simpson and Paul Tonta... and, it goes without saying, thanks to the filmmakers, without whom this book would be full of blank pages.

Dedicated to my Uncle Ross, who opened my eyes to the wonderful world of movie monsters.

Contents

CONTENTS

'Monster Mash'
(1962)
Song by Bobby 'Boris' Pickett

I was working in the lab late one night
When my eyes beheld an eerie sight
For my monster from his slab began to rise
And suddenly to my surprise

He did the mash
He did the monster mash...

Where the Wild Things are…
An Introduction to this Guide

'Monster. noun. an imaginary creature that is typically large, ugly and frightening. Origin late Middle English: from Old French "monstre", from Latin "monstrum" – portent or monster. From "monere" – warn' – definition of 'monster' from *The New Oxford Dictionary of English* (1998)

Dear Reader,

Since the dawn of time, monsters have existed in storytelling in pandemic proportions. In whatever form they may appear, these beings are the physical manifestation of our subconscious fears, anxieties, paranoias and other primal impulses – the 'id' rising up to bite us on the collective bottom.

The moving picture has enabled the mythical monster to experience 'life' in a way that goes beyond crude cave drawings and fantastical illustrations. With the invention of celluloid and a phenomenon known as 'creature features', monsters found a means to stomp around, roar and terrorise the bejesus out of living/breathing people/actors. Through film, the monster has truly come into its own.

This Pocket Essentials book is intended as a passionate introduction to the Monster Movie; a broad cross-section of films from the past 100 years of cinema, lovingly selected by a discerning author based on two important criteria – quality of movie and quality of monster – and should be viewed as a springboard into fervent investigations of the genre. However, this (small) book is NOT a definitive guide to the Monster Movie. No matter what an author may say, such a book is yet to exist, and it would require a series of encyclopaedic volumes to do justice to the subject.

So how does one recognise a Monster Movie? How have the 70 or so films detailed in this book been identified as Monster Movie-worthy?

Many people consider the Monster Movie to be a B-movie, predominantly those of the 50s and 60s, often heavily influenced by science fiction. This book takes a much wider perspective on Monster Movies, expanding the definition to include any film that hinges on a monster of some persuasion; hence vampires, werewolves and zombies also make the grade. Films featured are more of the horror, sci-fi or cross-genre persuasion, though, which explains why G-rated, kid-friendly monster movies like *Shrek*, *Teen Wolf* or *Monsters Inc* have not made the cut.

Rather than examine work according to a chronological history, the Monster Movies have been categorised under their 'monster type', followed by a further dissection of 'physicality' and 'personality' for specific monsters under the featured films. Some monsters could feasibly fall under two or more monster types but, for argument's sake, one dominant type has been chosen under which any particular monster sits. This is the final word – further justification will not be entered into.

Apart from this author's own incessant yammerings, seven

esteemed filmmakers have shared their mutual love for Monster Movies in a series of interviews that book-end each monster category/chapter of this guide. As film craftspeople with extraordinary imaginations and insight, their observations are the colour and light in what would otherwise be a one-sided appraisal – and, for their extraordinary visions (both here and in film), I am eternally grateful to each and every one of them.

No monsters were harmed during critical dissections, although I now require a nightlight at bedtime, a cup of warm cocoa and the reassurance only a plastic mattress protector provides. As the following pages will divulge, movie monsters are everywhere and they are here to stay. You have been warned…

Monstrously yours,

Emma Westwood

P.S. Feel free to write to me at the following address:
pocketessentialmonstermovies@gmail.com

Watch Those Chemicals! Big Monsters that Stomp on New York and Other Cities

With feet that have the footprints of trucks and hands that crush cars like cans, big monsters create pandemonium wherever they venture without even trying. Concocted from nuclear fall-out, toxic compounds or even extinct species plucked from their habitats, these monsters are a rude awakening about man's responsibility when it comes to volatile substances. Hazchem = handle with care.

King Kong (1933)

Director: Merian C. Cooper & Ernest B. Schoedsack, USA

Unlike Dracula and Frankenstein, King Kong stands alone among monsters, Merian C. Cooper creating him purely for the screen – and not from a literary work. That said, Cooper did draw inspiration from the swashbuckling jungle adventures of Arthur Conan Doyle and Edgar Rice Burroughs, and makes more than a token gesture to *Beauty and the Beast*; something that's reinforced continually through the dialogue. As the opening card so eloquently states:

14

'And lo, the beast looked upon the face of beauty. And it stayed its hand from killing. And from that day, it was as one dead.'

As a director of only a few features, nothing in Cooper's career would come close to the monumental success of *King Kong* and, quite frankly, he really didn't have to prove himself after this movie. It is a film that is much bigger than its monster. Even watching *King Kong* today is an exhilarating experience, although Fay Wray – a 1930s idyll with thinly drawn eyebrows, tight Cupid's-bow lips and platinum-blonde curls – would have contemporary feminists cursing at her pronounced fragility. She even lies prone and powerless as Kong cheekily peels off her clothes(!).

But all political correctness aside (and who needs it anyway?), *King Kong* is an excellent premise, well executed, that has given us one of cinema's most recognisable moments – a daring Kong dangling from the top of one of New York's iconic edifices with a Barbie–doll-sized woman in his hand. From *Q – The Winged Serpent* (p.20) to *20 Million Miles to Earth* (p.152), many a film has paid homage to this denouement.

Despite impresario Carl Denham being one of the dodgier characters in the movie, especially in Peter Jackson's version, he was apparently a fictionalised version of Cooper, who was quite the Indiana Jones–type crusader. On bringing Kong to New York, Denham bills him as 'The Eighth Wonder of the World'. When Cooper penned that now famous tag, could he have fathomed his ape creation would take on such proportions?

'It wasn't the airplane,' says Denham at the film's conclusion. 'It was beauty who killed the beast.'

Physicality: Essentially a very big gorilla, King Kong didn't require much imagination to sketch into details. He is an abomination of nature existing in a prehistoric world held in stasis, and probably would have lived out a relatively charmed life if it wasn't for the intrusion of those pesky filmmakers.

Coming off another prehistoric feature, *The Lost World* (p.28), 'chief technician' Willis O'Brien was ready to leave the world gasping in awe with his complex stop-motion fighting sequences between Kong and the other carnivores on the island – see Kong rip open the jaws of a T-Rex for a particularly grisly moment. While Kong is the feature attraction, the dinosaurs act as some impressive back-up dancers, particularly the Loch Ness-like creature rising up from the water through the mist. Stunning.

Personality: Considering the island natives regularly sacrifice their women to keep Kong at bay, he's obviously a prickly personality – and one they choose not to know better.

But as demonstrated by Kong's soft spot for blondes, his aggressive projection does not run through to the core. Under that thick, fur coat beats a sentient heart, and one that proves his downfall in the game of survival in what would become renowned as cinema's most heartbreaking instance of unrequited love.

Important to note is that, from start to finish, in the original film, Fay Wray is completely petrified of Kong and maintains the back-of-hand-to-brow histrionics right through to his swan dive from the top of the Empire State Building. Peter Jackson's most recent re-imagining of the film opts for a stronger relationship between Beauty and her Beast (among other things), to the point that she actually chooses to scale buildings with him and gaze lovingly into those dark eyes beneath his monkey brow.

Lineage and Legacy: Good golly… Where does one start? Actually, the question should be, what would cinema be like WITHOUT *King Kong*? Stretching infinitely beyond the somewhat limited categorisation of 'monster movie', *King Kong* created the template for the 'adventure film', which means the careers of George Lucas, Peter Jackson and Steven Spielberg would have been markedly different without its influence.

The great Ray Harryhausen attributed his viewing of *King Kong* at age 12 to changing the course of his life, propelling him into the intricate world of stop-motion animation. Without Harryhausen's enterprising work (*The Seventh Voyage of Sinbad*, p.23), cinema would not have had the special-effects foundations that gave rise to such mega hits as the *Lord of the Rings* trilogy… In short, *King Kong*'s tentacles stretch into every nook and cranny of cinema.

As most people will be aware, *King Kong* has been remade twice to great fanfare (in 1976 and, the longest version, in 2005) and has undergone numerous sequels, starting with *The Son of Kong*, which was released in the same year as the original film.

The beauty of Kong, although he is 'the beast' of the tale, is that he is so transportable and timeless. He's tackled Godzilla (*King Kong vs. Godzilla*, 1962). While in Japan, he also fought with his steel-clad doppelgänger, Mechani-Kong (*King Kong Escapes*, 1967). And he even earned himself a British clone (*Konga*, 1961).

When it comes to *King Kong*, there are few films that can

boast such transcendence and vitality that they live outside of their own confines. Would most kids know where that Donkey Kong computer game got its name? Actually, they probably would. That's the thing about *King Kong*.

The Host (2006)
aka *Gwoemul*

Director: Bong Joon-ho, South Korea

The highest-grossing film ever in South Korea, *The Host* is one of the most important, if not *the* most important, monster movies of recent years. Yep, it's a goodie.

Even though filmmaker Bong Joon-ho says he pitched at realism (like the monster in *Alien*) and, consequently, created a creature on a smaller scale, this part-fish-part-reptilian amphibious mutation is large and toxic enough to sit within our 'Big Monster' category. In fact, true to the template of the classic mutation, this 'host' was born from a cocktail of chemicals irresponsibly poured down a laboratory sink (at the insistence of an American official – read the politics here) and was based on a real-life incident.

Not only do the fish go belly-up and grow into weird forms, but this one particularly aggressive aberration takes to the land and collects a fleet of people on which he feasts, or just dumps in his nest for later. Subtlety isn't his bag, as is demonstrated when this monster first appears on a gloriously sunny afternoon in one of the best monster reveals ever committed to celluloid.

The cumbersome creature awkwardly slips and stumbles, careening through the mayhem of panicked picnickers, snap-

ping up a victim here and there to drag along. Most signifi-
cantly for this story, though, he chooses the daughter of a
dysfunctional family and, from here on, the drama turns into
that of a kidnapping where the family fight to save their little
one, rather than battle the Goliath-like monster on a hero's
journey. They are losers, so we kinda like them.

Far removed from the Hollywood system, *The Host* was
filmed in the actual sewers of the Han River. The cast and
crew were told they were receiving tetanus vaccinations, but
were actually being immunised against more dangerous para-
sites, like blood-sucking tapeworms that live in rotting
cadavers! In this hellhole of an environment, they
constructed a superb piece of monster cinema, as entertaining and comical as it is poignant in its depiction of a
flawed family unit.

Physicality: In describing the monster, Bong Joon-ho
believes he would be in constant pain, such is the hideous
assemblage of his body. He is a cross-mutation between a fish
and reptile, which means he has legs for the land and a tail
for swimming in the water, but the packaging of these body
parts is without Darwinian logic. The skin is eel-like and his
mouth open likes a ferocious flower, some might say resembling female genitalia.

As has been the case with many legendary monsters, *The
Host* took its cues from prehistoric forms (in other words,
dinosaurs) and was designed to be 'slightly dull and bulky'.
One of the monster's early incarnations included a second
parasitical creature living under the top layer of his skin,
feeding from his brain through a straw-like tongue.

Personality: Just as the chemicals have mutated his body, they have also messed with his mind. This monster is a scatterbrain in the extreme sense – volatile and confused. He works on instinct, his survival mechanisms mature enough to see him create a home to store his 'food' and to rest. But this is all basic stuff. He is just a simple being.

Lineage and Legacy: At this premature point in time, it's difficult to ascertain what the legacy of *The Host* will be. However, based on the film's earning potential alone, it seems likely it will spawn an army of imitators. Surprise, surprise – a Hollywood remake is in the pipeline.

While director Bong has ruled out his participation in a sequel, *The Host* is just too good to be put to bed at this early stage in the cinematic 'raping and pillaging' process. There's still more originality to be milked from this sucker.

Q – *The Winged Serpent* (1982)

Director: Larry Cohen, USA

One thing about Larry Cohen: he's a brilliant writer (check out 1976's *God Told Me To* for another startling example where similar parallels between gods and monsters are drawn). Despite Q being pulled together at a moment's notice – Cohen started shooting within seven days of being sacked from directorial duties on *I, the Jury* – it's a super-smart monster movie. From the opening sequences, where a pervy window cleaner gets his head spectacularly lopped off and blood starts raining down on the heads of unsuspecting pedestrians, you know you're in for a lot of fun.

Just as King Kong scaled the Empire State Building, Q makes the spire of the Chrysler Building her nest. Stealthy and swift, this giant 'plumed serpent' takes the inhabitants of the city unawares, swooping down on topless, rooftop sunbathers and picking off construction workers for a midday snack. The appearance of the giant Q coincides with a curious spate of ritualistic killings where the victims are flayed.

Not only does Q make the Big Apple her home, this film really *owns* the city. Whirling over the skyscrapers of Manhattan in a helicopter, Cohen beautifully captures the vibe of a seedier metropolis – pre-Giuliani – when the twin towers of the World Trade Centre are still standing and organised crime is more prevalent on the streets.

Cohen rarely shot with permits, so the stunned looks of passers-by in the 'Neil Diamonds' robbery sequence are the genuine looks of citizens, not extras. Apparently, David Carradine agreed to star in the film without having read the script and Michael Moriarty, working under the same conditions, pulls off an intense and wonderfully erratic performance as a petty thug.

Q is, quite simply, inspiring filmmaking.

Physicality: Q, or Quetzalcoatl as the Aztecs knew him, is a very, very large Mexican feathered serpent. Considering the film was made on a tight budget, pulled together by a series of favours, the various effects that created Q are a bit clunky, to say the least – Cohen even filmed the blue screens in his own home. But this doesn't detract from the appeal of a large claw snatching its feed or a glimpse of this prehistoric creature, with its lizard-ish body and head, flying freely over the city. According to facts on birds, Q would be six-times stronger than a man of her size.

How could a monster like Q go largely unnoticed, you ask? Well, according to the police officers investigating the crimes, she flies in line with the afternoon sun so that anyone looking overhead is dazzled by the sky's brightness. A nifty bird indeed.

Personality: Conjured by fanatics of Aztec culture, Q is supposedly a deity, although David Carradine's character is sceptical – 'It wouldn't be the first time in history that a monster has been mistaken for a god,' he says.

Legend has it that Quetzalcoatl is an Aztec sky and creator god whose name is a combination of 'quetzal' – a brightly coloured Mesoamerican bird – and 'coatl' meaning 'serpent'. He is the most well known of Aztec deities and is commonly thought of as the principal Aztec god, even though he comes from a pantheon of gods where none is considered superior to the others.

As such, Q is accustomed to getting her way and thinks she has the run of this city. When it comes to people, she views them as little more than her next meal. Appropriately for a god, she chooses the Chrysler Building as her home – a grand example of art deco architecture with eagles protruding from its façade. In other words, Q is a special bird so any old edifice will not suffice.

Lineage and Legacy: In creating Q, Larry Cohen references a number of films, including *King Kong* (p.14) and other mammoth monster movies like *The Beast from 20,000 Fathoms* (p.89). However, as far as the wider consciousness goes, Q seems to largely fly under the radar. Hopefully, in books like this one, we can keep the legacy of wonderful movies like Q – *The Winged Serpent* alive.

The Seventh Voyage of Sinbad (1958)

Director: Nathan Juran, USA

Even though Nathan Juran (*Attack of the 50 Foot Woman*, p.177) wears the badge of 'director' with *The Seventh Voyage of Sinbad*, the film's branding is very much that of special-effects wiz Ray Harryhausen, who is one of the few film craftspeople considered an auteur of his work. This goes to show the extent of Harryhausen's influence and that of the many mythical, stop-motion creatures he created over a long career.

The first colour pic from Harryhausen, featuring a memorable score by composer Bernard Herrmann and the first appearance of one of Harryhausen's signature creations (the living skeleton – see also *Jason and the Argonauts*, p.31), this film is held in great affection by Baby Boomers, who had their imaginations indulged by the film's assortment of wondrous monsters. Ask someone about early cinema experiences and, more often than not, *Seventh Voyage* rates a mention, its melding of mythical storytelling and cutting-edge special effects (for the time) the stuff of childhood fantasy.

Utilising what he termed 'Dynamation – the new miracle of the screen', Harryhausen pioneered stop-motion animation. He said, 'Stop-motion, to me, gives that added value of a dream world that you can't catch if you make it too real.' Working without an assistant, he painstakingly moulded all his models and then photographed them one frame at a time to create the illusion of movement. For *Seventh Voyage*, this laborious animation process took him 11 months to complete.

Rather than present just one monster, *Seventh Voyage* serves up quite a few as obstacles to Sinbad, the hairy-chested sailor from the famous Arabian Nights tales, in his quest to save his princess. Read on…

Physicality: Harryhausen loved contrast, which meant many of his monsters were large, overwhelming their foes in a David-and-Goliath kind of way. In *Seventh Voyage*, these beasties included a blue-skinned, multi-armed serpent woman (formerly the princess's handmaiden), a two-headed Roc (gigantic bird), a dragon chained in a magician's lair and, most predominantly, a pissed-off Cyclops.

Emerging from a stone mouth on the beach on the island of Colossa, the Cyclops is hoofed, with furry goat's legs, and stands on two feet. He is undoubtedly the most beloved creature from this film; Harryhausen, however, reportedly preferred his serpent woman, conceived after watching a performance by a real belly dancer in Beirut.

Personality: Hardly any of the monsters featured in Harryhausen's movies are friendly. Most of them act as guardians or protectors of some form of treasure and therefore possess an aggressive nature, similar to that of an attack dog.

Cyclops is no exception. When Sinbad and his minions land on Cyclops's beach, he does his best to scare them away or tear them to bits. When they don't take the hint, he roasts them on a rotisserie like stuffed pigs.

Lineage and Legacy: *The Seventh Voyage of Sinbad* is the first and most popular film from Harryhausen's Sinbad trilogy that includes *The Golden Voyage of Sinbad* (1974) and *Sinbad and the Eye of the Tiger* (1977). It also marked a major turning point in the careers of Harryhausen and producer Charles H. Schneer, allowing them access to the mainstream and, consequently, bigger budgets.

In terms of influence, *Seventh Voyage* – and, in fact, Harryhausen's body of work in general – has affected possibly every science fiction/fantasy filmmaker since in some way, either as fans or as craftspeople themselves. The special-effects techniques perfected by Harryhausen have been used in a wide variety of films over the years, surpassed only recently by CGI – although, for some, Harryhausen's style is still far more beguiling.

Ray Harryhausen has attributed his interest in stop-motion to watching *King Kong* at age 12. He would go on to earn his filmmaking stripes on *Mighty Joe Young* in the 40s.

Cloverfield (2008)

Director: Matt Reeves, USA

Comparisons between *Cloverfield* and *Godzilla* (p.92) are not without justification. In fact, just as the Japanese used *Godzilla* to try to come to terms with the nuclear destruction of their cities over half a century ago, America now has a film through which it can purge 9/11 paranoia.

Producer J.J. Abrams, of TV's *Lost* fame, says, 'Having a movie that is about something as outlandish as a massive creature attacking your city allows people to process and experience fear in a way that is incredibly entertaining and incredibly safe.'

Abrams came up with the idea for *Cloverfield* during a trip to Japan when he realised that America was lacking a culturally enduring monster, such as Godzilla is to modern Japanese folklore. The time seemed ripe for the invention of such a creature; however, the story needed some sort of contemporary element to cement it in the 'now'. Enter a new age in consumer technology.

In terms of storyline, *Cloverfield* doesn't break any new ground, but what makes it a monster movie for the twenty-first century is the way it is executed. The assault of the creature – whatever it is – on New York City is relayed through video cameras, mobile phones and other such communication devices, as captured by Joe Blow public. Everyone is as clueless as the next person about what's happening – very similar to that experience of watching New York's World Trade Centre towers crumble to the ground.

As Abrams explains, 'So much of what's conveyed in real amateur or documentary footage is what you hear but don't see – the panic and reactions to what's happening off-camera and the sounds of things you don't see. At the end of the day, we wanted to feel like anybody with a camera could have made this movie.'

Physicality: Just as Godzilla bore a resemblance to T-Rex, the monster in *Cloverfield* looks like a derivative of some sort of prehistoric beast, although its centre of gravity is closer to the ground – more crouched as opposed to walking on hind legs.

It's a little difficult to lock on to its actual size; however, it is definitely big. It also carries smaller parasitical monsters that occasionally jump off and do some solo scavenging work.

As an audience, we're afforded very little further information, but that's the point. We need to piece together details from what's being talked about on the street, from people just like us who are spouting all sorts of nonsense and Chinese whispers. Government conspiracy, anyone?

Personality: In creating the monster, J.J. Abrams admits to wanting something 'insane and intense' rather than a cuddly King Kong character. But then the special-effects supervisor, Phil Tippett, talks about the monster as a childlike character suffering from separation anxiety. Whatever this monster may be, he's not visiting Manhattan to make friends, that's for sure.

Lineage and Legacy: *Cloverfield* was sure to be a 'monster' hit thanks to a cleverly devised viral marketing campaign that had everyone downloading teasers of this untitled new film from the Internet. The dangling of this carrot generated big profits.

Despite direct links to *Godzilla*, it would be surprising if *Cloverfield* could grow legs like its Eastern counterpart and wreak havoc for 50 years. As fun as it is, it does feel like a one-movie experience, but time will tell...

And Then Some...

The Lost World (1925)

Director: Harry O. Hoyt, USA (silent)

Long before *Jurassic Park* (p.29), or even Ray Harryhausen, *The Lost World*, based on Sir Arthur Conan Doyle's book, resurrected dinosaurs through such revolutionary achievements in special effects that the film is now considered 'culturally significant' by the Library of Congress in the USA.

If *The Lost World*'s importance was ever in doubt, its trio of big 'firsts' should provide evidence enough: it was the first live-action dinosaur flick, the first film that combined stop-motion with living actors and the first among several adaptations of Conan Doyle's book.

A specialist in recreating prehistoric existence on screen, Willis O'Brien's stop-motion effects with *The Lost World* would prove a vital warm-up for his more famous work – *King Kong* (p.14). But, for the record, there's nothing inferior about his effects here. Just as King Kong was suspended over New York, the climactic sequence of this film, where a dinosaur stomps through London, is legendary stuff. Reportedly, at the time, a test reel of triceratops, allosaurus and stegosaurus had the Society of American Magicians fooled, which even included Harry Houdini.

DVD releases of *The Lost World* offer extra footage spliced from prints over the years, but the film can also be viewed (and legally downloaded) on the Internet, as it is now part of the public domain.

MONSTER MOVIES

Jurassic Park (1993)

Director: Steven Spielberg, USA

Based on the Michael Crichton novel of the same name, *Jurassic Park* sees director Steven Spielberg flexing his muscles with regard to new technology. The story follows a team of scientists as they converge on a remote island where an amusement park is being established for a genetically cloned species of formerly extinct dinosaurs.

Combining the talents of Stan Winston's studio and George Lucas's Industrial Light and Magic (ILM), Spielberg created a showcase for how good special effects can be – and one that, surprisingly, has remained largely unsurpassed over the last 15 years.

Whereas so many productions now rest on their CGI laurels, *Jurassic Park* pedantically drew on the strengths of a variety of techniques and merged them into a stunning whole. Digital computerised effects – which could be a little 'unorganic' in close-ups – were used for full-body dinosaurs and movement. Body parts and full-screen close-ups were usually achieved with a puppet created by Stan Winston's workshop.

Best viewed in its big-screen celluloid glory, *Jurassic Park* was a huge box-office success and the sequels – two at current count (the first of which was also directed by Spielberg and borrows its title from the earlier film *The Lost World*) – just keep on coming, with *Jurassic Park IV* slated for 2009. *Jurassic Park* reminds us that, while computers may be cool, a little bit of old-fashioned imagination goes a long(er) way.

Them! (1954)

Director: Gordon Douglas, USA

One of the first (and some might say finest) 'animal muta-
tion' films released as a direct result of nuclear paranoia,
Them! has stood the test of time and was, deservedly, Warner
Bros.' biggest hit of 1954. Whereas many other 'big' films, like
Attack of the 50 Foot Woman, were experiments in schlock,
Them! is serious stuff.

Presented in a semi–documentary style, the FBI and police
are baffled by the disappearance of several people in the New
Mexico desert. After analysing a strange print found at one
of the crime scenes, they uncover a strain of giant mutated
ants, which are the product of the first atomic-bomb explo-
sion. Destroying the nest is the least of their worries – it's
containing the winged queen ants before they establish more
nests that tests the authorities in a race against the clock.

While *Them!* may sound hokey – I mean, giant ants? –
Gordon Douglas's presentation of the script is serious, even
sombre. Of course, Dick Smith's giant ant models aren't as
impressive as they were 50 years ago, but they're part and
parcel of the complete package of this moody and atmospheric monster flick.

If you're going to limit yourself to watching just one of the
nuclear monster films, then you'll be well served by putting
Them! at the top of the list.

Jason and the Argonauts (1963)

Director: Don Chaffey, UK/USA

Colourful and epic in every way, Ray Harryhausen once again takes us to an ancient world where gods messed with the fate of mortals like pieces in a chess game. In this case, Zeus and his lady friend Hera have taken an interest in Jason, who collects a crew to sail to the ends of the Earth in search of a magical golden fleece.

Along the way, he tackles a creaking, bronze colossus called Talos that moves like a skyscraper, but easily straddles the bay with his two legs, which makes giving their ship a shaking a piece of cake. There are also some blue-winged harpies; a massive half-man, half-fish god, Triton (the only big monster that's a huge human projection rather than stop-motion animation); a seven-headed serpent called Hydra (reputably a bitch to animate as Harryhausen didn't have the luxury of video playback to record the directions in which the individual heads were moving); and one of Harryhausen's best achievements, his skeleton army.

Not to be missed.

Gamera (1965)

Director: Noriaki Yuasa, Japan

It's heartbreaking not to be able to do justice to all the wonderful *Kaiju Eiga* films over the past half-century of Japanese cinema, but there are only so many films that can be squeezed into a pocket book. So take note: the big three of

Godzilla (p.92), *Mothra* and *Gamera* are some sizeable muthas that are also must-sees.

Gamera was produced by *Godzilla*'s rival studios, Daiei Motion Picture Company, where the character would star in a stream of films that helped him gain a level of notoriety as a Japanese icon. Essentially a giant flying turtle, Gamera possesses the non–turtle-like qualities of being able to stand on his hind legs, the ability to withdraw his limbs into his shell and take off into the air, and a mouth full of extremely large teeth, including a pair of tusks jutting out from his lower jaw.

As with Godzilla, Gamera's revival was the result of a nuclear blast, this time in the Arctic where dogfights were taking place between US and Russian fighters. In the original *Gamera* film, his awakening sends him on a journey to Japan where he decides to rip up some buildings and proves too hardy even to suffer a scratch at the hands of modern weaponry – as tends to be the case in these giant Asian monster stories.

This is just a nibble at the cake when it comes to learning about Gamera. Don't just nibble, though – take a big bite.

From the Desk of...
Roger Corman
(USA)

'What is Jaws, *if not a Roger Corman movie on a big budget?'* –
New York Times

Filmography: As a producer, Roger Corman has made 380 films and, as a director, 55, including: *The Day the World Ended* (1955), *It Conquered the World* (1956), *Attack of the Crab Monsters* (1957), *Not of this Earth* (1957), *Wasp Woman* (1960), *The Little Shop of Horrors* (1960), *The Masque of the Red Death* (1964), *Frankenstein Unbound* (1990), *Carnosaur* (1993), *Dinocroc* (2004)

Monsters tap into an innate human fear. I feel that this all boils down to simple evolutionary biology. This morbid interest in and fascination with monsters certainly has its roots in the early days of our species.

As it goes, of course, early humans who were smart enough and fast enough to escape the larger and dangerous creatures survived and passed on their genes. What's more is that those clever enough to pass on the stories of these terrible creatures are the ones that ultimately propagated the race because their communication of fear and survival intelligence allowed them to continue their genes. It would follow that the human race should be populated by those predisposed to this trait. Monster stories are very important to the human psyche in an intensely intimate and primitive way, and I believe that explains much of why these pictures are so immensely popular with audiences today.

I think that monster pictures and horror pictures, in general, reflect the changing socio-political climate and that is what audiences have always responded to enthusiastically. Social climate has everything to do with what audiences are looking for and what they respond to in motion pictures. But also, what's 'always scary' is what is always possible.

For example, after World War II ended, there was a flood of pictures that focused on some type of creature that had been transformed by some nuclear accident. The nuclear threat during those years became an unavoidable part of the public consciousness and there was a new kind of fear that was influencing the public, not only across America, but across the world.

In many of today's monster movies, we see creatures that are born out of genetic manipulation or unethical practices in advanced DNA technology and bioengineering. This is also evident in the movies where the monster is not a creature at all, but some advanced and uncontrollable AI. These are realistic concerns exaggerated into a palatable form of entertainment. Like the early humans warning through stories of dangerous monsters, these films offer a sort of self-aware and prophetic warning to our culture.

There are many different recipes for creating a terrifying monster. To summarise, I try to create monsters that are both frightening and a little sympathetic. This can truly catch an audience off guard and introduce a level of complexity and depth that captures and intrigues people in a very special and endearing way.

In addition to this, I try to show the monster in only bits and pieces while establishing the story and being ever so careful not to reveal too much of the monster too soon. Suggestion can be one of the greatest tools of building suspense. Also, this method can play to the individual in a very effective way. By revealing the monster gradually, the horror of the film interacts with the individual psychology of each member of the audience. The result of this allows a personalised experience that can be far more frightening than anything I could create.

There will always be something new when it comes to monster creations. With the current rate at which special-effects technology is progressing and all of the headway that has been made in this field, I believe there is no limit to what sort of creatures will come into being through the coming generations of storytellers.

I also believe, echoing what I said before, that changes in society will certainly influence the evolution of monsters in film. Although different archetypes are sure to appear, I feel they will continue to be based upon fundamental fears within us, though the external will take on different appearances. Of course, the social and political circumstances of the future will most likely inform the nature of these creations and, therefore, it can be difficult to predict what monsters will come next.

Frankenstein's monster is one of my all-time favourite monsters. Aside from being adapted from a true masterpiece of literature, the picture really created the model for the sympathetic monster that I work from to this day. Another picture that I have greatly admired is *Alien*; however, more so as a pure horror film. This picture embodied the techniques of effective suspenseful storytelling and creating a compelling monster. *Alien* truly seemed to ring in the modern movement of creature design.

If I had to pinpoint favourite monsters from my body of work – and it's tough to narrow this down – I'd have to say the creature from *It Conquered the World* and also *Attack of the Crab Monsters*. I'd have to say *Carnosaur* too – that one ranks near the top – and another would be *Dinocroc*.

Out of all of my films, though, my absolute favourite monster would probably be the creature from *It Conquered the World*. Because of my background in physics, I have always tried to design these creatures from a logical perspective. I figured that a monster from Jupiter, subject to the intense gravity on that planet, would probably be very low to the ground. So, following this logic, I had the creature built about three feet high.

Right before we were about to roll, Beverly Garland, who was starring in that picture, walked over to the monster and kicked it, and said something like, 'Conquer the world, will ya!' I understood what she meant, so I stopped the scene and instructed the prop master to make the monster at least 12 feet tall. I gave him until after lunch and rearranged the shooting schedule for that entire morning to allow time for the monster to be made larger. Finally, we ended up with an insane-looking conical addition to the top of the creature. From that point on, I've always started with one principle: the monster must always be bigger than the leading lady.

Given the opportunity to make another monster movie, I

would love to do a shape-changing monster. A creature like this would always have the audience surprised. In every scene, there would be a new and more terrifying monster than the previous.

In addition to shock, a monster that shape-changes would hold the audience in extended suspense and terror because they would truly be at a loss as to what was coming next. A shape-changing monster embodies the fear of the unknown and would certainly keep audiences screaming.

It's Alive... Alive!
Man-made Monsters

This collection of mad-scientist films shakes the finger at man's aspirations to play God or improve on nature, cinema's moral comment on 'enhancement' gone wrong. As you will see, the ability to engineer life and create superior beings does not necessarily result in perfection. It's more likely to incite mayhem of the most unsightly variety, as these gothic (or neo-gothic) tales of hubris and compassion demonstrate.

Frankenstein (1931)

Director: James Whale, USA

When Mary Shelley first penned *Frankenstein* (or *The Modern Prometheus*) in 1818 as part of a literary parlour game with her husband and Lord Byron, she could not have fathomed the 'monster' she had created. Her story became the stuff of literary legend and almost immediately made the leap from page to stage then screen (as soon as the technology was made available).

Frankenstein is indisputably the benchmark for all mad-scientist stories, made even more pertinent today by the prevalence of plastic surgery and recent debates concerning cloning and genetic engineering. At the time, it echoed the plight of World War One veterans who, physically as well as mentally scarred, were seeking acceptance and assimilation into an unforgiving society.

An early film incarnation of *Frankenstein* is Thomas Edison's 16-minute, silent production of 1910, but it wasn't until James Whale's *Frankenstein* in 1931 that the Monster took on a physical appearance that would sit at the height of public consciousness for generations to come. Originally, Béla Lugosi, hot off the success of Universal Studios' monster hit *Dracula*, was coined to step into the Monster's shoes, but Lugosi felt the layers of makeup would hinder his looks and performance. Serendipity saw the deeply chiselled and statuesque Boris Karloff win the role and, quite literally, the rest is cinema history.

So enigmatic and sympathetic was Karloff's portrayal – without dialogue, only through grunts and groans – he created a monster that people came to regard with considerable affection. It is also testament to his brilliance that the name 'Frankenstein' was largely attributed to his character, which was actually nameless, rather than the scientist Dr Frankenstein (Colin Clive) who plays the titular role.

First-time viewers of *Frankenstein* may experience a sense of having 'seen it all before', such is the film's cultural dominance – we *feel* like we've seen it, even if we haven't. Not only that, but there is a naïvety to the movie that makes the warning at the beginning seem more amusing than threatening.

At the time of its release, though, the imagery in *Frankenstein* was legitimately disturbing – cadavers, hypodermic syringes and terrorised expressions – despite coming across as G-rated today. Some prints of the film removed the scene where the monster throws a young girl into the lake to ascertain whether she floats, as well as Dr Frankenstein's proclamations of feeling like God. To that end, the film's 'warning' was Universal's protection against the ire of church groups.

Frankenstein utilises the long shadows and exaggerated depth of field of German expressionist cinema. Most notable is the burning windmill of the film's finale; it's a stunning set piece, made all the more menacing by the lack of any music bed, not to mention the bobbing flames on stakes and dog barks from a pursuant lynch mob. This is a film to be considered in its own historical context, but, nonetheless, a monster that cements the importance of the monster movie itself.

Physicality: Thanks to the skills of Jack Pierce, then chief makeup artist at Universal, Frankenstein's Monster is one of the most recognisable cultural icons of the twentieth century – the deeply chiselled lines, padded-out brow and heavy-lidded eyes (which were enhanced at the request of Karloff to make the monster look more lifeless), built-up boots, electrodes at his neck (often mistaken for bolts by the audience), the sunken cheeks (achieved by removing a dental plate) and, of course, that distinctive flattened head.

Pierce's makeup took hours to apply and – a mix of cotton collodion, gum and green greasepaint to create a sullen pallor on the black and white film – was uncomfortable in its application and removal. Karloff indeed suffered for his art every day on set. Despite his strength and mammoth build, the final scene where he carries his creator up the windmill resulted in three back surgeries and ongoing pain for the rest of his life.

Regardless, Karloff appreciated the importance of Frankenstein's Monster and never regretted the typecasting such a role inevitably imposed on him.

Personality: Frankenstein's Monster inherits the brain of a killer, which some people believe undermines his innocence, so that, theoretically, his first instinct is to inflict harm. Yet, Karloff plays him more like an empty vessel, the patchwork man whose reanimated brain acts solely on impulse, floundering in a world where everything is alien, just like a newborn baby.

Most telling is the Monster's scene with the child Maria, with whom he instantly develops a rapport and who, despite being much younger, finds herself in the position of teacher. This is the only scene where the Monster expresses delight by smiling and bouncing in excitement, like an over-enthu-siastic puppy dog. For the rest of the movie, he stumbles around on a search for acceptance.

Lineage and Legacy: It goes without saying – *Frankenstein's* legacy is a massive one. So many films are indebted to Mary Shelley's original premise and so many films still ride on the coattails of the *Frankenstein* movie moulded by James Whale.

In one of the first nods to movie sequel-dom, *Frankenstein* (1931) was followed by *Bride of Frankenstein* (1935), *Son of Frankenstein* (1939 – the last to star Boris Karloff as the Monster), *Ghost of Frankenstein* (1942), *Frankenstein Meets the Wolf Man* (1943 – with Béla Lugosi finally playing the monster role), *House of Frankenstein* (1944), *House of Dracula* (1945 – in which Frankenstein's Monster makes an appear-ance), *Abbott & Costello Meet Frankenstein* (1948), Andy Warhol's *Flesh for Frankenstein* (1973), Roger Corman's

Frankenstein Unbound (1990), the blaxploitation film *Blackenstein* (1973), a string of movies focusing more on the creator than the monster from Britain's Hammer Studios... and this is just the tip of the iceberg.

As can be surmised from this modest list, *Frankenstein* progressed from pure terror to pure farce in many cases, although the general concept of 'Frankenstein' insidiously infiltrated cinema and has cropped up in a number of films in different disguises, (see *The Fly*, p.48, and *Re-Animator*, p.52).

Anyone enamoured with *Frankenstein* would also be well served to check out Bill Condon's fictionalised drama *Gods and Monsters* (1998), which depicts an aged and ailing James Whale recalling key moments from his life. Whale's tortured history and his repressed homosexuality informed themes of 'normality' in *Frankenstein*, which is popularly considered to have had an impact on the historical development of the 'camp' monster movie, like Mel Brooks's *Young Frankenstein* (1974) and *The Rocky Horror Picture Show* (1975).

Bride of Frankenstein (1935)

Director: James Whale, USA

Just as *The Godfather: Part II* is to *The Godfather*, *Bride of Frankenstein* is one of the few sequels that (arguably) eclipses its original. Director James Whale was hesitant to commit to the project at first, but on the prompting of the studio, Universal – which granted him the type of creative licence usually reserved for independent filmmakers – produced what many consider his masterwork, a horror movie that is witty and emotional in equal parts.

Even though Mary Shelley never wrote about the Bride, the Monster's mate was part of her vision and, consequently, Whale orchestrated a fictional prologue with Shelley, her husband and Lord Byron setting the scene. Those with a keen eye will note that Elsa Lanchester, who later appears as the Bride, doubles here as Mary Shelley.

A new 'mad scientist' character is introduced this time round – the delightfully loony Dr Pretorius, played by Ernest Thesiger, who was Whale's mentor in real life and reportedly as eccentric as his character – to coax the psychologically volatile Henry Frankenstein into joining him in his quest for 'a new world of gods and monsters'. After showing Henry his people 'miniatures' – a great example of early special-effects cinematography by John J. Mescall – he hatches a plan to create a female 'life partner' for the Monster.

Meanwhile, Frankenstein's Monster lumbers around unfettered causing havoc wherever he appears, but largely reacting against the hysteria. Not surprisingly, the locals continue in their vengeance and he fights for his survival, despite eventually admitting, 'I love dead, hate living,' once he gains the power of speech. Apparently, Boris Karloff, who reprised his role as the Monster, believed that talking would stymie his performance. However, Whale's decision prevailed and proved correct.

While the Monster's language may be limited, he manages to say a lot, especially when he meets a blind hermit, played by O.P. Heggie, who is the only person who extends to him the hand of friendship. Through his new friend, he receives love, lodging, food and music, as well as a few perfunctory words – 'good', 'bread', 'wine', 'smoke' and 'friend', among some others.

Sitting at the heart of the film, this seminal scene, although a little melodramatic for a modern audience, is the key to finally establishing the Monster as a sympathetic character. If ever his sentience was under question, we now see him as a basic man who, through his innocence and confusion at the world, appears more compassionate than any of the villagers calling for his death.

If only all sequels were this good.

Physicality: No doubt nourished by his success in *Frankenstein*, Boris Karloff returns as the Monster, although less gaunt than before. Jack Pierce's makeup is unchanged, except for some singeing of the Monster's hair and burns to his face, acquired whilst crawling out of the fire at the end of the previous movie.

Frankenstein's Bride takes the cake as the only iconic female monster in cinema history. She begins existence like an Egyptian mummy, swathed in bandages from head to foot, before being jolted to life through a lightning strike.

In contrast with her male counterpart, though, Pierce endeavoured to ensure actress Elsa Lanchester's good looks shone through her makeup, especially important for the series of jump cuts that introduces her. The only mutilation is scars to her jaw line and neck.

Swathed in white, she also cuts a striking figure – all the more recognisable for her wacky hair style with white, zig-zagged curls up the sides, which, in another nod to Ancient Egypt, recalls the queen Nefertiti. The hairstyle was achieved by blending Lanchester's own hair with a wig around a wire cage propped on her head.

Personality: Frankenstein's Monster undergoes his strongest character arc in *Bride of Frankenstein*. By the conclusion of the film, he's not only communicating through speech, but making decisions based on intellect and reason, rather than instinct alone.

On the other hand, his Bride, newly animated, is an empty vessel, wary of everyone and everything, including her monster mate. When she screams, it's with a rasping kind of hiss – something that Lanchester mimicked after witnessing swans protecting their cygnets. Her appearance in the film is important, but brief, so we know very little about her, other than that she is extremely scared and defensive. Of course.

(Note, in Franz Waxman's Wagnerian score, in which he attributes leitmotifs to the various characters, the first three notes of the Bride's theme are the same as the first three notes of the Rodgers/Hammerstein song 'Bali Hai' from *South Pacific*).

Lineage and Legacy: See *Frankenstein*.

Dr Jekyll & Mr Hyde (1931)

Director: Rouben Mamoulian, USA

Out of the several screen versions of Robert Louis Stevenson's classic novel, Rouben Mamoulian's *Dr Jekyll & Mr Hyde* remains by far the most salient.

Not only is Hyde a memorably simian-like character (created by makeup artist Wally Westmore and played by Fredric March), but the groundbreaking filmmaking techniques used to transform him from the mild-mannered Dr Jekyll (pronounced 'gee-kl') were kept under wraps by Mamoulian for many decades – apparently, a series of rotating filters were attached to the lenses and matched to March's makeup. In terms of effectiveness, especially in the transformation from Jekyll through to Hyde rather than vice versa, Mamoulian's trickery is truly remarkable.

Released before the Hays Code cleaned up on-screen sauciness in Hollywood, *Dr Jekyll & Mr Hyde* was noted for its overt sexual content, particularly through the character of the prostitute, Ivy Pierson, played by Miriam Hopkins, who swings her gartered leg suggestively and beckons the good doctor to return some time.

Rightly so, Fredric March was honoured at the 1932 Academy Awards for his split-personality performance, but elephant stamps should definitely go to Hopkins, whose terrorisation at the hands of Hyde sees her employ varying levels of hysteria.

As Ivy Pierson so precisely puts it, 'He ain't human – he's a beast.'

Physicality: While Dr Jekyll may be suave and dapper, Mr Hyde is anything but. As Jekyll's primal self, Hyde is, appropriately, one seriously hairy chap with tombstone-like teeth filling out a crooked smile. His brow line is low, his nostrils permanently flared and his face prone to uncontrollable ticks.

Jekyll is very streamlined in physique, but Hyde puffs out his clothing and seems to degenerate into further unruliness as the film progresses, appearing to everyone as some sort of out-of-place monkey man, sipping on champagne in his top hat and tails.

Personality: Well educated and ambitious, Dr Jekyll is the kind of guy any father would be proud to wed to his daughter. Or not. When Jekyll courts Muriel, his frustration heightens because of her father's unjustified insistence that they hold off the wedding date. This makes Jekyll feel angry and, as any impatient scientist would do, he seeks to separate out this deplorable side of his personality.

Welcome Hyde – all the base instincts and irrationality of Jekyll packaged up in the one hirsute being, without love and objectivity acting as dilution. Hyde is an irrational maniac who takes out his frustrations and sadism on the poor, deprived Ivy.

Lineage and Legacy: This Jack the Ripper-style tale boasts an enviable legacy, so strong that referring to a 'Jekyll/Hyde' personality has entered into our everyday vernacular. Similarly, such a strong story concept was never going to stop with just one movie.

Given the opportunity to run through all the Jekyll/Hyde adaptations on film, television and in literature, we'd be here for an eternity. However, attention should be drawn to the Spencer Tracy version of the film, produced in 1941, directed by Victor Fleming and placing Ingrid Bergman in Miriam Hopkins' celebrated role.

As was done to *Frankenstein*, comedians Bud Abbott and Lou Costello decided to have a farcical go at it with *Abbott & Costello Meet Dr Jekyll & Mr Hyde* (1953).

The Fly (1986)

Director: David Cronenberg, UK/Canada/USA

A remake of the far camper, 1958 Vincent Price-starrer of the same name, Cronenberg's *The Fly*, produced by Mel Brooks, is a heart-wrenching love triangle (Jeff Goldblum, Geena Davis and John Getz), although seasoned with nerdish sci-fi overtones, as well as a chilling reminder of our inevitable deterioration as human beings.

While the original monster was, effectively, a man with a gargantuan fly head and fly hand, Seth Brundle aka 'Brundlefly' – the successor – begins as the classic mad scientist, plagued with motion sickness and, therefore, prompted to create a motion-free transporter. When a humble housefly surreptitiously joins him in one of his telepods, the computer fuses the two entities together, and so begins Brundle's eventual subjugation to the fly's DNA, with him acting as commentator to his own monstrous transformation. To heighten the emotion, Cronenberg pitches at real insect characteristics, drawing from his interest as a junior entomologist when he was a youngster.

Both *Fly* movies are drawn from the short story by George Langelaan, published in a 1957 issue of *Playboy* magazine, that may not have been magical in its prose, but gave birth to a premise so strong its influence would inform two films decades apart. It also cemented Cronenberg as an auteur of 'body horror' (see *The Brood*, p.172).

Physicality: Tall, dark and magnetic, Brundle begins as a nutty loner immersed in his world-changing experiment who then reaches out to a female journalist in his desperation to share the dream. Once Brundlefly comes into being, he slowly takes on the appearance of a 185-pound fly, which culminates in the shedding of any Homo sapiens body parts, such as ears, teeth and fingernails (he stores them in the bathroom cabinet, something he affectionately refers to as 'The Brundle Museum of Natural History').

Completely CGI-free, Brundlefly (created by Chris Walas Inc) is, essentially, a man in a rubber suit, but played for realism as opposed to Godzilla-esque kookiness (the film also won an Oscar for makeup effects). By the time Brundlefly takes his final bow, only his eyes reflect a glimmer of the humanity from which he came. He is frighteningly real and powerfully plausible – in shots where puppetry was utilised, puppets were built to human scale.

Personality: Brundle is initially buoyed by the vim and vigour he experiences with the fly developing within him, although he is unaware of his synthesis with this fly. Cronenberg uses the idea of the fly DNA as an amphetamine, like the 80s *drug du jour* cocaine: Brundle craves sugar, his sexual potency increases; he becomes unfathomably strong and agile, and quick to snap to irritability and agitation. One of the nauseating characteristics of Brundlefly is his need to cough up an acidic fluid for digesting food. As the 'experiment' develops, he captures these distinctly fly-like habits on video camera with the aid of his love interest, Veronica.

In one of the film's central monologues, as he learns more about his new self, Brundle tells Veronica, 'Insects don't have politics – they're very brutal, no compassion, no compromise. We can't trust an insect… I'll hurt you if you stay.'

Lineage and Legacy: Brundlefly is a one-of-a-kind movie monster, conjured via experiment and never to be repeated. A box-office success, Cronenberg's film did spawn a sequel – *The Fly II*, starring Eric Stolz, which admittedly does propagate the Brundlefly bloodline – although, as is the case with many movie franchises, very little of the brilliance of Cronenberg's work spilled over into it. Interestingly, Cronenberg's special-effects guy, Chris Walas, is the director.

To this day, Jeff Goldblum's idiosyncratic portrayal of Brundlefly – horrifying yet remarkably personable and consistently humorous in the face of his own dreadful decline – is a triumph in acting through layers of latex and slime. Although *The Fly III* never reared its ugly head, yet another remake is on the cards.

The Invisible Man (1933)

Director: James Whale, USA

For this author, *The Invisible Man* is the most interesting of Universal's classic monster movies and the best showcase for James Whale's talents as a filmmaker. Stacked with trick effects and a sinister mix of black humour and evil, it's the kind of film that, even 70-plus years after its original release, retains its sense of vitality. There's a definite 'wow' factor in the highly imaginative invisibility effects by John Fulton.

Taken mainly from the H.G. Wells novel of the same name, *The Invisible Man* introduced British actor Claude Rains to American audiences, largely through a commanding vocal presence. Considering his character is… well… invisible, Rains' central performance was bound by bandages, eyewear, or not being there at all. Such restraints could have proved detrimental to the film, but Rains rose above his restrictions to create a mad scientist fuelled by malevolence and Machiavellian notions of power.

The details of this film are wonderful: take, for example, when the Invisible Man runs through the intricacies of his transparency, where undigested food, dirt under his fingernails and even fog could give him away. The beautifully choreographed chase sequences combine slapstick hilarity with sheer frustration – he sends grandfather clocks toppling in his wake, beers sliding across the bar, steals bikes and makes a mockery of police dragnets, literally pulling the rug out from under them.

Physicality: You can't see him so, physically, he's only as good as the suit he's wearing and some snazzy sunglasses.

Personality: Talk about ego – Jack Griffin, our invisible man, is so full of himself he starts buying into his own grandiose notions of invincibility. As far as he's concerned, everyone else is a mere plaything, an annoyance, a blip on his radar. They may try to trap him, but he is considerably more intellectually advanced than them – even the boys in blue, who he continually ties in knots.

Considering he holds the undying devotion of a lovely woman, we can only assume that Griffin was once a nice guy, before the monocaine – a drug from India, which is the secret ingredient to the invisibility formula – started messing with his mind. Even he admits: 'The drug seemed to light up my brain. Suddenly, I realised the power I held, the power to rule, to make the world grovel at my feet.'

Lineage and Legacy: Like all good monsters, Universal milked *The Invisible Man* movie for all its worth with a number of sequels – *The Invisible Man Returns*, *The Invisible Woman*, *The Invisible Agent*, *The Invisible Man's Revenge*, *Son of the Invisible Man*.

Trivia point: take a good look at Gloria Stuart as Flora, who will be recognisable to audiences from her Oscar-nominated role in James Cameron's *Titanic*.

And Then Some...

Re-Animator (1985)

Director: Stuart Gordon, USA

If ever a tongue-in-cheek homage to *Frankenstein* was created, then this film is it. *Re-Animator* was director Stuart Gordon's first film and the beginning of his love affair with adapting the literary works of H.P. Lovecraft – a gross-out example of a *Frankenstein* offshoot taken to black comedic extremes.

Jeffrey Combs plays the Lovecraft character of Herbert West, a precocious young scientist who creates a serum that can bring the dead back to life. As would be expected, things go belly-up when delusions of grandeur push him into dangerous territory.

Following some hilarious experiences 're-animating' a black cat, the film descends into the depths of gore – murky territory that's designed for a definite cinema clique who are tickled pink by severed body parts and bucket loads of exposed intestines. All this builds to a wonderful climax where a lecherous character literally loses his head.

In the words of film critic Roger Ebert, this is 'a livid, bloody, deadpan exercise in the theater of the undead'. And, predictably, there's also *Bride of Re-Animator* (1990), directed by Gordon's producing partner, Brian Yuzna. Enough already.

Black Sheep (2006)

Director: Jonathan King, New Zealand

Debut feature filmmaker Jonathan King introduces us to a brand-new monster breed – killer sheep. First thoughts are this is probably just a big bag of farce, but think again. Lightning paced, genuinely funny and sodden in splatter (beautifully generated by Weta Workshop), this is a super-fun comedy/ horror hybrid, a genre that's been hitting its stride with the likes of *Shaun of the Dead* (yeah, there's a pun in there).

Set in King's homeland of New Zealand – the joke being New Zealand is famous for its abundance of sheep (40 million, give or take a million) – the 'black sheep' of the story have been genetically mutated by a group of bio-engineers, employed by a malicious property owner to create a deluxe breed of animal.

This is a new instalment in the New Zealand tradition of gross-out/comedy/horror hybrids made famous by Peter Jackson, who then went on to bigger budgets with the likes of remaking *King Kong* (p.14). A fluttery 'baa' never sounded so menacing...

The Killer Shrews (1959)

Director: Ray Kellogg, USA

Falling squarely in the 'so bad, it's good' category, *The Killer Shrews* sees a group of incongruent people on a remote island tackling a pack of... yep... killer shrews, the by-product of experimentation into creating a race of small humans to counter over-population (interesting logic).

Ironically, this was the first film directed by Ray Kellogg, who would carve out a career as a respected special-effects artist – ironic because the 'special' effects in this chuckle-a-thon are woeful. As far as the untrained eye can tell, these supposedly bloodthirsty shrews are nothing but some waggy-tailed collie dogs trussed up with fluffy rugs tied to their backs. Groovy.

Fiend Without a Face (1958)

Director: Arthur Crabtree, UK

It's interesting how some films – great in their corniness – hold a dear place in the hearts of cinemagoers for generations to come. *Fiend Without a Face* is one such film.

With unsubtle studio lighting and drama that unfolds as though along the 180-degree axis of a theatrical stage, the greater portion of the film sees the characters endlessly discussing what might possibly be occurring. As far as action goes, it all kicks up several notches in the last 15 minutes of the movie, which is when the previously invisible fiends take on a visible form as disembodied brains with dangling spinal columns.

Despite a lack of legs or wings, these mutant brains manage to sail gracefully through the air, attaching themselves to the backs of people's heads where they suck nourishment and consequently render their victim dead. However, they're still vulnerable to bullets – and go down with a thick sounding 'glug glug' or 'ffp ffp' noise.

There are definite similarities between *Fiend Without a Face* and *Forbidden Planet* (p.145) – although *Forbidden Planet* is the more accomplished of the two – which will go unexplained here so as not to sabotage the viewing experience. Enough said. Watch them both and see for yourself.

House by the Cemetery (1981)

Director: Lucio Fulci, Italy

Lucio Fulci is one of those controversial filmmakers, praised as much as he is lambasted. Quentin Tarantino even cites him as a major inspiration and acquired a beautiful copy of Fulci's film *The Beyond*, which this author was privileged to behold.

The name 'Fulci' goes hand-in-hand with gore – so be prepared before renting one of his films (think: woman hucking up her own intestines). And *House by the Cemetery* is no exception. It sees a family move into a spooky house that is (three guesses) situated by a cemetery. What they don't realise is that an eccentric nineteenth-century physician called Dr Freudstein had been conducting illegal experiments there, and continues to reside in the basement in a ghastly, zombified, sub-human form (zombies are a Fulci specialty e.g. *Zombie Flesheaters*). Freudstein keeps his body functioning by supping on fresh flesh.

Fulci is as subtle as a sledgehammer – for instance, is there any subtlety in calling your character 'Dr Freudstein'? Some may derive more laughs than artistic appreciation from a Fulci film, but still, when it comes to Italian horror cinema, he sits alongside Mario Bava and Dario Argento as a luminary in his chosen field. Pop him on your list.

From the Desk of...
Adam Simon
(USA)

'Steven Spielberg spent $47 million building his dinosaurs, while Roger Corman spent about $47 on Carnosaur... *Carny, as we call him, is like a midget Godzilla with a lethal lizard tail, but the scariest thing about him is that he grins exactly like Barney the Dinosaur. Look at THAT while he's chomping your gizzards. Even Raymond Burr would give up.'* – Joe Bob Goes to the Drive-In (16 July 1993)

Filmography: *Brain Dead* (1990), *Carnosaur* (1993), *The American Nightmare* (2000)

As a filmmaker, I think horror is one of those forms – monsters, in particular – that people select early on, or it selects them. Mysteries are a bit that way too, in the way that the people writing them or making them tend to be great consumers of mysteries to begin with, which isn't true of all genre forms.

The documentary I made, *The American Nightmare*, was partly an attempt for me to answer the question: why was it that at the age of 8 through 12 – an age when you're most receptive to ideas – I was drawn to horror movies? Who knows? People can go off with a whole lot of psychological ideas of why.

Almost every kid goes through a stage of liking dinosaurs or enormous creatures. There's certainly something that comes from the experience of being a small creature in a world of large, powerful, dominant giants that have control over your fate. I think some movies – and this applies more narrowly to monsters than to horror in general – often play with issues of scale and size. That might seem obvious, but we underestimate the fact that our sense of the world comes from our embodiment within it and, not only do we begin very small, but we begin in a state of almost constant meta-morphosis. We experience our bodies in all kinds of bizarre ways as children and we are – in a way that we never will be again – surrounded by other members of the species that are of a vastly different size. That, in itself, is somehow monstrous.

So it's very natural that kids are drawn to stories about dwarves and elves and giant creatures. It makes sense. People look at this stuff as if it's the opposite of realism and it's not. It's quite realistic from the point of view of a kid, in all kinds of ways.

Probably not coincidentally, before I even finished film school, Roger Corman – one of the masters of the monster movie – pulled me out of film school and signed me up to a three-picture writing-directing deal with him. I almost immediately started making horror movies, including what was probably his final and ultimate monster movie, *Carnosaur*.

For better and for worse – maybe it would have been better for me if he had not – he sent me on a certain path, just at a moment in the early 90s when that kind of B-film-making and having that kind of filmmaking as your background, unbeknownst to all, was about to lose its cachet. And this was after having been the key first step for almost every American director of any worth of the previous generation.

Roger said to me, 'Adam, you should be very proud. You've made one of the best films I've ever produced and you've made the most profitable. Unfortunately, they're not the same film.' One was *Brain Dead* – which he really loved and was one of the last films he produced that got him acclaim for actually being a good movie, and then the other was *Carnosaur*, which was... you know... not by any measure a great movie.

Because *Carnosaur* was made for so little, and under particular circumstances, it was made with technology that was very, very primitive at that time. Literally, it's everything from forced perspectives and hand puppets to guys in rubber suits. It's got a little bit of everything in it, but it's fun.

One of the things Roger was very smart about doing was capitalising on certain kinds of movies when they were coming out. In this case, he knew well in advance about *Jurassic Park* because he had been a friend of Michael Crichton for years. And he knew this would obviously be a big movie. So the idea was to piggyback on the vast advertising budgets of these bigger movies – get awareness because of theirs.

Roger had bought a truly, truly terrible – though fun and funny – novel called *Carnosaur* by a guy who wrote under the pen name Harry Adam Knight – the first letters of which spell 'HAK'. It was actually John Brosnan, who'd written a lot of non-fiction books on horror movies. Anyway, Roger had bought *Carnosaur* and figured that he'd use that as the basis for his movie *Carnosaur*. When he brought it to me, he said,

'Don't read the book. I just want the title – I like the title – and I just want the protection of it having been a book.'

I think I've failed some parts of my own test with *Carnosaur*... I don't think we have much, if any, sympathy for the creature. In the original movie (there were sequels too), we just have this one dinosaur that escaped from the experimental facility he'd been developed in. But I have to say, I don't think he offered much of the pathos or character quality that Godzilla has – he just doesn't have that much personality. I think Diane Ladd, who plays the mad scientist, does a lot of good things in it, but I don't think the creature himself is very interesting. Roger is being self-serving to say *Carnosaur* is one of his favourite monsters. It's not on my list of favourite monsters, I can tell you that.

The prerequisite of a monster movie is a monster. The question is: what's a monster? A monster is, by definition, something that is unnatural. Here's one way to look at it: the word itself has roots in the idea of something to be seen or to be shown. It is related to words like 'prodigy' – not in the sense of an intellectual prodigy, but of some kind of unnatural birth, for example. It's very related to the things you might have seen at a freak show, for example.

The monster is a survivor. It's a holdover from the pre-Copernican world. It's a holdover from the world when magic still lived, when the Earth was at the centre and not the sun, when we didn't have the rules of physics and science. It's a survival of the images from fairytales, from mythology, from nightmares into what has otherwise become a reasonable world.

The same creatures who, for you and I, are monsters, when they show up in Homer, they're not monsters – they're creatures and they're creatures to be dealt with, but one doesn't spend a lot of time saying, 'Oh my God, how could such things be?!' When Ulysses and his men are stuck on the Cyclops island, they're not spending any time asking, 'How the hell did this thing get here?' They accept that there's this creature with one eye that's probably descended from some god and they're going to have to kill it and get away. But, 800 years later, if I'm going to write a story about that thing, it's become a monster. A Cyclops in Homer is not a monster. He's a Cyclops, because he actually fits into their natural order, which includes gods and creatures of all kinds.

The monster is precisely an artefact of the Age of Reason. It is a survivor of the Age of Unreason into the Age of Reason. In the Age of Reason, we continue to tell stories about monsters because we still need those creatures – we still love those creatures – and we even sense somehow that those creatures are true, even though they don't fit into our grid any more. So, in fact, we create for them a new space in our grid, defined precisely as that 'that doesn't belong here'.

If you go back through the Greeks and the Romans, let alone every other culture that ever existed, you will find everything we've ever considered to be a monster. You will find vampires, you will find werewolves... even Godzillas. You'll find them all. But they're not monsters then. They belong there. The key line in any monster movie is the people saying 'this thing doesn't belong here' or, in some cases, very poignantly, the creature itself – like in the case of Frankenstein and his bride saying, 'We don't belong here, we belong dead; this isn't our world.'

Part of the problem of saying Hannibal Lecter is a monster is that humans lose part of the real poignancy of the monster.

In every monster movie, there's a moment of poignancy in relation to that monster because it doesn't belong. That's why we can have a strange kind of sympathy for Godzilla or for King Kong – and even for the vampire, sometimes. We often expect science fiction to take care of that, rather than treat it in the realms of horror. Monsters, especially from the 1950s, have lived more in science fiction than in horror.

There's a moment in the evolution of horror – and that moment is *Psycho* – when the whole style and the whole idea of what is a realistic monster shifts and basically shifts to human monsters. To that extent, every psycho killer movie could be said to be a monster movie. But I think 'monsters' is absolutely the wrong word for that.

Films like *Wolf Creek* and, for that matter, *The Texas Chain Saw Massacre* going back all the way to *Psycho*, are absolutely horror movies and teeter on the edge of being fairytales, of being somehow impossible, but they're so grounded in the real. The questions they raise are about the extremes of the human psyche and of why evil exists, but they never quite cross 'the cosmic line' of the real and the beyond. The monster is really part of that other thing – the beyond.

In my list of favourite monster movies, I'd have to include the original *King Kong*, although I'm a huge fan of the Peter Jackson one too. For some reason, every true lover of monsters has a particular affection for the idea of a giant gorilla. No one can be quite sure why that is, but I'm sure there's again a deep psychological evaluation for the appeal of that figure. Again, it's a survivor... it's a survivor from this other era.

I'd have to say that I'm a bit of a classicist. I like the Universal monster movies – *The Wolf Man*, *The Mummy*,

Dracula. I'm not a big fan of the *Creature from the Black Lagoon*, I must admit. *Creature from the Black Lagoon* is a great example, though, of the monster as a survivor from one kind of paradigm into another. I really love *The Wolf Man*. I really love the werewolf and all kinds of shape-shifting creatures like that.

Each one of these represents one of the fundamental archetypes of the monster. There is the King Kong-type monster that is literally the survivor from another time. There is the shape-shifter monster, who is fundamentally a human being, but who has become another creature. The vampire is, along with Frankenstein, the monster in relation to death – it's the monster as immortal – and 'immortal' is inherently a monster, which is a very powerful idea.

I think people often miss what is monstrous in the vampire. They focus on the fact that they have fangs or they drink blood or you can't see them in the mirror. No, what is fundamentally monstrous about vampires is their immortality. Frankenstein is this other thing: a man-made monster. Not monster as a man, but the monster that a man makes, which is a very particular and powerful kind of monster too. And that's about what happens when humans try to be God. The difference is, we can create, but our creations will inherently be monsters. That's the difference between us and God.

As a kid, one of my favourite monster movies – and a category unto itself – was the movie *Freaks*. I saw it at that same golden age of horror – aged 10 or 12 – that I saw *Frankenstein*, *Dracula*, *The Wolf Man* and *The Mummy*. I remember seeing *Freaks* and being absolutely riveted – horrified – but it also has all the elements of sympathy that a true monster movie should bring up.

This idea of the freak is a key because, in fact, if you were to go back and ask 'where does this whole monster thing come from?', a lot of it comes from monstrous births that were somehow viewed as portent signs. The word 'monster' in our common language tends to come from that — a freakish birth — which was taken to be a sign.

What the word 'monster' really means is 'a living sign'. It means a 'monstrum'. It's closer to the word 'demonstrate' than it is to 'creature' and that is because it was assumed that these prodigies — these horrific births — were cosmic signs. They somehow carried with them something of the divine. So there's this key connection whereby this grotesque frightening thing — whether it be a two-headed cow or Siamese twins — is somehow connected in the human mind with the divine. I'm quite certain that this is where our idea of the monster, and even the term as we use it, originates.

There's no such thing as a monster in a world where the supernatural is the natural — there's no need for the category. You just have to know what to do when you see one.

Hubble Bubble, Toil and Trouble...
Demonic Monsters

They have evil as their intent. They are demons, witches, cursed souls and possibly even the Devil himself in whatever guise he chooses to appear. As all God-fearing citizens know, dabble with the dark side and you risk being pitched into the fiery depths of hell. The power of Christ compels you...

The Exorcist (1973)

Director: William Friedkin, USA

Cinema doesn't get eerier than *The Exorcist*. I guess there's something intrinsically disturbing about seeing a 12-year-old girl spin her head 360 degrees, spit out sacrilegious profanities and pea-soup-green bile, and masturbate with a crucifix...

Based on William Peter Blatty's 1971 novel of the same name, this film is not only accomplished in its depiction of a possessed being – pushing acceptability in a way cinema had previously not dared – it is also purportedly taken from documentation of a real exorcism performed on a young boy in 1949. Just as ouija boards and pagan ritual are deemed dangerous territory, no matter what your religious persuasion, watching *The Exorcist* is somehow dirty business. It really does get under your skin.

Despite its controversial content, *The Exorcist* went great guns at the box office and was nominated for ten Oscars, of which it won two (Best Sound and Best Adapted Screenplay), which probably says more of the social climate of that time compared to our current age of conservatism, particularly in terms of faith.

As a film, it meanders at a rather slow and meditative pace – not a bad thing at all, but something that could test the attention span of a different generation. A significant proportion of the plot is concentrated on the back-story of the two priests, although it is the imagery of a possessed young Regan MacNeil (portrayed by Linda Blair in a role that would colour the rest of her career) that has captivated viewers.

Interestingly enough, it was rumoured that Stanley Kubrick was approached to direct the film; however, the task eventually fell in the lap of William Friedkin, who was flying high on the success of *The French Connection* (and who would later direct a severely underrated remake of *The Wages of Fear* – *Sorcerer* – which arguably presents another marvellous cinematic monster in the form of a beastly truck, but I digress...).

Whether most people are drawn to *The Exorcist* out of morbid fascination or what, this film is so potent – so worryingly real and emotional – that it deserves being the top-grossing R–rated film of all time.

Physicality: Regan starts the movie as the ultimate golden child. She's the apple of her mother's eye (Ellen Burstyn), and so sugary sweet that butter wouldn't melt in her mouth. In fact, she's a little too good to be true, as we discover.

Her possession begins with some small behavioural problems, such as peeing on the carpet at her mum's party, but quickly catapults into a state of decline that sees her roped to the bed at all times. The old Regan is trapped deep within her body, communicating via distressed messages carved into her abdomen, while another someone, who claims to be the Devil himself, uses her as a conduit to the earthly world.

The 'Devil' is abusive in many ways, not excluding Regan's body, which falls into disrepair the longer her 'guest' stays with her – her lips crack, her breath becomes laboured and vile, her skin seems to rot. With a little help in the special-effects department by Dick Smith, she's not looking so good any more.

Personality: This monster is big on personality, although not one you'd like to have around. He relies on verbal manipulation to attack his enemies, picking at the priests' mental vulnerabilities, which consequently erodes them both physically and psychologically.

He is smart. Really smart. He knows how to twist conversations and confuse people. Still, he has his weak points too, as the lacerations caused from holy water prove.

While this demon has a lot to say, casual discourse with him is not recommended. His words are cruel, his abilities boundless, his motivations pure evil. In other words, nothing good is going to come from a pow-wow with this hellish creature.

Lineage and Legacy: It probably goes with the territory of a film about demon possession, but *The Exorcist* has been the stuff of urban legend with many a cast and crew death linked to the production, as well as other strange happenings.

While that's all hearsay, Friedkin has been accused of unwarranted audience manipulation through the use of subliminal imagery, such as 'Captain Howdy', a demon face that is flickered on-screen at various points for nothing longer than a frame, which is meant to register on the viewer's subconscious mind only. Friedkin released a longer director's cut of the film (an excellent one too) that includes more graphic medical testing on the sickly Regan, as well as a 'spider walk' sequence where she contorts herself backwards and creeps down the staircase.

The film's sequel, *Exorcist II: The Heretic* (1977), is an odd film; director John Boorman was unable to replicate the 'feel' created by Friedkin, but nevertheless managed to collect a cult of loving fans. The third film, *Exorcist III* (1990), directed by the novel's author William Peter Blatty, is surprisingly good, despite being far removed from the original – more crime thriller than anything else.

Mention 'demon possession' and all thoughts will turn to *The Exorcist*, such has been the legacy of this film. Not only have there been many spoofs (*Repossessed* anyone?) but also made-for-TV versions and foreign-language rip-offs, such as a Turkish film called *Seytan* (1974), which has been criticised for being a scene-for-scene remake.

Night of the Demon (1957)

Director: Jacques Tourneur, UK

An enduring horror movie with a complex, mystery-based storyline, *Night of the Demon* is the work of director Jacques Tourneur, who is primarily known for the atmospheric

chillers he created with producer Val Lewton in the 1940s –
Cat People (p.174), *I Walked with a Zombie* and *The Leopard Man*. While Tourneur breaks free of Lewton here, there are many stylistic and thematic consistencies, most notably Tourneur's ongoing fascination with the supernatural.

Based on the 1957 book *Casting the Runes* by M.R. James, *Night of the Demon* stars Dana Andrews as the ever-sceptical-in-the-face-of-general-weirdness American psychiatrist, Dr Holden. On arriving in the UK to speak at a conference debunking witchcraft, Holden investigates the mysterious death of a British colleague and, in the process, has the date of his own death predicted by a self-professed warlock.

While the bulk of the film involves the bull-headed Holden refusing to budge on his own beliefs during his investigation into satanic practice, it is book-ended with a fabulous monster – a demon that emerges from the trees and through swirling clouds of wind. We see very little of this demon – what little we do see is still much more than Tourneur intended, though – yet the demon dominates the entire narrative and, as a result of its overriding threat, propels the story to a genuinely climactic close.

With its long shadows, eerie darkness and power of suggestion, *Night of the Demon* is definitely a horror movie, but one that appeals to those who prefer their horror diluted with plot rather than thickened with gore.

Physicality: Dragon-like in appearance, this gargantuan demon manages to drift in the night sky, light as a feather despite its hefty size – large, clawed feet pedalling the air – never touching the ground. Its preference is to emerge from

the treetops in a misty cloud, swooping down on its proph-
esised victim from above.

It is widely reported that Jacques Tourneur wanted to
apply the 'less is more' theory to showing his demon, but the
producers of the film inserted tacked-on close-ups to tie in
with poster and day bill artwork. Unfortunately, these static
shots of a cheap puppet head looking directly into camera,
with rolling eyes and lolling tongue, only lessen the impact
of these important moments in the film. When compared to
the long shots, they are, in fact, even inconsistent with the
demon's physical appearance.

Personality: Considering it appears only at the moment of
death and for one reason – to kill – there is little we know
about this demon, except that it has no mercy.

Lineage and Legacy: When initially released, *Night of the
Demon* took a backseat to Hammer's *The Revenge of
Frankenstein*, with which it screened as part of a double-bill
feature. Ironically, among film pundits today, Tourneur's little
flick enjoys the greater repute of the two, considered by
many as one of the best supernatural horror films ever to be
made. It was even deemed worthy of a 'making of' book
called *Beating the Devil: The Making of Night of the Demon* by
Tony Earnshaw, published relatively recently in 2005.

(Be wary: *Night of the Demon* is more widely known by its
American release title, *Curse of the Demon*, although the
'curse' version is a good ten minutes shorter).

In popular culture, *Night of the Demon* has been referenced
by the likes of Kate Bush in her 1985 track *Hounds of Love* –
'It's in the trees! It's coming!' – and also in the opening song

from *The Rocky Horror Picture Show*, where there is a line that goes, 'Dana Andrews said prunes gave him the runes, but passing them used lots of skill.'

The Mummy (1932)

Director: Karl Freund, USA

Moving through this movie like a tall, priestly statue, Boris Karloff is simply magnificent in *The Mummy*, the most understated of Universal's stable of classic monster films. This might be early cinema, but few images have been as powerful as this centuries-old mummy's eyes flickering open for the first time; a gesture so slight, but one that easily trumps the uninspiring CGI effects of its recent versions.

Stepping up to the directorial chair for his debut with this film was cinematographer Karl Freund (*The Golem: How He Came into the World*, p.76), already a name at Universal for his camerawork on *Dracula* (1931), as well as for shooting Fritz Lang's sci-fi masterpiece *Metropolis* (1927). This is not the only similarity between *The Mummy* and *Dracula* – screenwriter John L. Balderston also wrote *Dracula* and imbued both films with concurrent themes of timeless love and a spellbinding monster.

The Mummy was, reportedly, close to Balderston's heart too, him having been a media correspondent at the opening of King Tut's tomb in 1922, which was the event that kick-started the West's love affair with anything Egyptian. As well as a fascination for Egyptian design, the concept of a possible mummy's curse was entrancing to a general public, enough to send this film to the top of the box office.

Physicality: For the most part, 'Karloff the Uncanny' is the fez-wearing, caftaned Ardath Bey, whose luminous and somehow lifeless eyes have the power to hypnotise. Universal's Jack Pierce applied layer upon layer of makeup over approximately six hours to create Karloff's stony complexion, in need of some heavy-duty nourishing moisturiser and reflected in his dry performance – dignified with very little vocal inflexion. The removal of the makeup was apparently an excruciatingly painful process for Karloff to bear.

Ardath Bey is merely a ruse, though, Karloff's true identity being the bandaged, ancient mummy Im-ho-tep, cursed and buried alive for sacrilege. Following his resurrection at the archaeological dig, he makes it his mission to reacquaint with his lost love, an Egyptian princess, reincarnated as a half-English, half-Egyptian woman, Helen (played by feisty stage actress Zita Johann, an ardent believer in reincarnation herself).

Personality: As the 'romantic' lead, Karloff is hardly the swooning Valentino. He comes across as strangely emotionless, as we could guess a resurrected, mummified human being would be, yet his motivation is for love and love alone. Considering this, he is the ultimate romantic, maintaining an emotional commitment that stretches for eternity.

Ardath Bey/Im-ho-tep is also incredibly intelligent and calculated in his efforts to achieve his purpose, despite being ruled by the heart over the head.

Lineage and Legacy: Karl Freund's vision of *The Mummy* was potent enough to inspire a legion of official (and unofficial) sequels – *The Mummy's Hand, The Mummy's Tomb, The Mummy's Ghost, The Mummy's Curse, Abbott & Costello Meet the Mummy* and a string of films by Britain's Hammer Studios.

If we were to believe superstition, even the productions themselves may have been 'cursed'. Most notably, the rumour mill turned over at Hammer when *Blood from the Mummy's Tomb* (1971) was being produced. Peter Cushing dropped out before filming when his wife became fatally ill and director Seth Holt died mysteriously following a case of the hiccups.

The moral to the story: don't mess with the dead, especially if they are wrapped in bandages and come from a mummy's tomb.

Suspiria (1977)

Director: Dario Argento, Italy

'Il Maestro' of Italian *giallo* horror, Dario Argento, scored his biggest hit in the United States with the atmospheric, supernatural thriller *Suspiria* from his witch trilogy – the others being the comparable and, in some ways, superior *Inferno* (1980) and *Mother of Tears: The Third Mother* (2007), completed 30 years after the first film.

While *Suspiria* may have given Argento a name of sorts in the US, he still remains on the fringe of Hollywood mainstream consciousness, yet in Italy he maintains a merchandise store and it's not unusual to hear his film themes as phone ring tones. He is also a repeat collaborator with George A. Romero in many different capacities.

Argento movies are an acquired taste, sometimes leaving

viewers cold due to the Italian propensity for cumbersome overdubbing and Argento's leaning towards 'style over substance'. But as far as this little black duck is concerned, Argento in his early- to mid-career prime is *the* shit.

A good widescreen (and uncut) print of one of Argento's classic movies is a goose-bump-inducing experience – listen for whispers layered beneath the soundtrack (more often than not composed by brilliant prog-rock band Goblin) and be hypnotised by pools of primary colour, expressionistic shadows and overblown set design. While it is debatable whether *Suspiria* is his best film, it is certainly a dazzling showpiece for Argento's signature style and a sexy exploration of the darker side of witchcraft.

The story goes as follows: young American dancer, Suzy, arrives at a prestigious ballet school in the German forest, only to be greeted by a distressed student. The student goes missing and it becomes apparent Suzy is out of step with the bitchy and elitist academy. Sensing danger, she does her best to avoid lodging on-campus, but finds herself forced into staying there. As more students disappear, Suzy discovers the ballet academy is a front for a far more sinister enterprise.

Physicality: The 'mother' of the *Suspiria* legend, the headmistress of the school – Helena Marcos – is a century-old witch, so her best days are now long gone. When she sleeps, it is with a painfully asthmatic wheeze and she largely slips through this film under a veil of invisibility. It is only in the film's finale that we're afforded a glimpse of her. And she looks as you'd expect a very old witch to look – like death warmed up.

This witch is bed-prone and has relinquished responsibility for wrongdoings to the more active witches in her coven i.e. the school's teachers.

Personality: Like all good cinematic witches, this woman is not very nice. Argento's witches are anything but sympathetic – *au contraire*, they are evil in its vilest form.

Considering Argento's penchant for slaying women – like Alfred Hitchcock – in increasingly gruesome ways, as well as his depiction of a variety of sadistic females, he's been accused by some of misogyny, although these are claims he hotly denies. While it all makes for entertaining cinema, *Suspiria* recalls paranoia of the fifteenth century and does little for the public image of those practising the tenets of Wicca.

Lineage and Legacy: While accumulating a legion of hard-core fans, Argento has produced very few imitators, possibly because *giallo* is a very subversive genre and Argento was one of the most internationally palatable directors of this form. Also, his films come alive through the filming, which leaves little in the way of screenplay to muck with for adaptation.

However, that said, there's been talk of a Japanese anime remake of *Suspiria* and he has inspired other art forms, including some rock bands who've named themselves and their albums after this history-making film.

EMMA WESTWOOD

The Golem: How He Came into the World (1920)

aka *Der Golem: wie er in die Welt kam*

Director: Carl Boese & Paul Wegener, Germany (silent)

With imposing sets, long shadows and moody underpinnings, *The Golem: How He Came into the World* is a marvel of expressionistic filmmaking, although its filmmaker, Paul Wegener, denied such intent.

Made at a time when cinema was yet to establish any solid precedents, the film's inception is a curious one: apparently, Wegener was so enamoured with the idea of Golem that he played the character himself (an imposing figure standing at six feet six inches) and made the film, not once, but twice, as well as a 1917 parody of the long-lost 1915 version of the film, which is (possibly) the world's first ever film sequel.

The story of Golem is a famous one, drawn from Jewish folklore, about a giant clay creature created by a rabbi in the sixteenth century to protect the people of Prague from persecution by the emperor. Some critics of the film have seen it as anti-Semitic, although others disagree.

Even though Golem is sculpted by hand, his life comes from the magic arts (rather than science), of which the Jews are depicted as masters. On the other hand, the Jews seem far more grounded than the emperor's knights – a pack of dandy-arsed wankers (take note of the flouncing Florian and the 'dancing man' who, startlingly, looks like he's hiding a ferret down his pants).

Physicality: The Golem is a big guy with large boots and a thick belt that cinches in his Santa Claus-like coat tightly at the waist. His face hides under a blocky-wig of a hairdo that is obviously solidified with the clay – in other words, his locks aren't blowing in the breeze.

On his chest, there is an amulet, which gives him his life force.

Personality: Apart from a few grunts, Golem isn't noted for his killer personality. He seems content to lumber around and spook a few people, but try and take his amulet and you might get a surprise – his will to live puts a spring in his step.

Lineage and Legacy: Take one look at Golem's stony expressions, rigid-limbed gait and raised footwear, and it's clear this silent European influenced one of the most influential monster movies of all time – *Frankenstein*. If such cross-continental links seem tenuous, then take heed of the film's credit sequence and you'll see a name that will be familiar from the American Universal Studios, Karl Freund, cinematographer on *Dracula* (p.128) and director of the Boris Karloff starrer *The Mummy* (p.71).

Comparisons have also been drawn between the 'creation' scene in *Golem* and that of F.W. Murnau's *Faust* (1926), as well as Golem and the 'Christianised' monster from Fritz Lang's *Metropolis* (1927).

Paul Wegener's name may not be at top of mind these days, but in the eyes of film historians he was a noteworthy contributor to the development of the German film industry and, consequently, the art of filmmaking as we know it today. Even though his oeuvre as an actor and director stretched far beyond Golem, he provided a face for this monster that would be his enduring stamp on cultural history.

And Then Some...

Hellraiser (1987)

Director: Clive Barker, UK

Sado-masochism is at the core of this deliciously over-the-top romp by author Clive Barker, adapting his own work. His otherworldly demons – called Cenobites – locked inside a box that gives new meaning to the Rubik's cube, are pinned, hooked, chained and peeled in a range of highly creative ways. And they're loving it.

As the story goes, a couple discover the hideous remnants of the wife's former lover in an upstairs room of their new home. A prisoner of the Cenobites, this unfortunate fellow is keen to rebuild his body, but needs the human sacrifices to do so.

Hellraiser has proved a great cash cow for its creator Clive Barker, extending across a string of sequels. As far as the Cenobites go, though, their leader, termed 'Pinhead', has developed a following that goes well beyond his role in the films. *Wizard Magazine* also named him the ninth Greatest Villain of All Time.

Jeepers Creepers (2001)

Director: Victor Salva, USA/Germany

General opinion is that *Jeepers Creepers* is just another teen horror film, but it really shouldn't be dismissed that easily.

Firstly, it turns most horror-movie conventions on their head – stuff like 'the preyed-upon couple have to be lovers' and 'the female is the most desired victim'. Even if viewers don't consciously know what these conventions are – or haven't seen *Scream* for these 'rules' to be spelt out for them – they'll have registered them subliminally.

Secondly, the 'Creeper' is spooky as hell – by day or night. A demonic being stalking people in the butt-crack of nowhere, he dresses in a trench coat and floppy hat to conceal his decaying form, feeding on human body parts to regenerate his own. Apparently, an organ from just anyone won't do – he sniffs out a liver here, a lung there, depending on the 'compatibility' of the donor.

Thirdly, if the Creeper doesn't scare you, his truck will.

Another interesting thing about *Jeepers Creepers* is that, as fun as it is, the sequel sucks hugely – and that's a sequel by the same writer-director.

Brainiac (1963)
aka *El Baròn del terror*

Director: Chano Urueta, Mexico

Executed by the Holy Inquisition of Mexico for a number of crimes (including seducing married women) in 1661, Baron Vitelius swears vengeance against the descendants of the inquisitors, which he achieves three centuries later in the form of a brain-eating monster. How does he return, you ask? In a comet, of course.

A marvellous oddity, 'Brainiac' looks like the old Baron for

most of the time; that is until the insatiable urge to suck
brains turns him into an enlarged, papier-mâché-like head,
that kinda pulsates, with a gigantic hook nose, unruly hair,
pointed ears and a forked tongue. He's so piecemeal, he looks
like he's been created as part of a secondary school craft
workshop. When he's not actively seeking out brains, the
Baron likes to keep them in a container, spooning out a
morsel as a between-meal snack.

A must for trash film connoisseurs.

The Evil Dead (1981)

Director: Sam Raimi, USA

Starring the wonderfully hammy Bruce Campbell, *The Evil
Dead* launched director Sam Raimi's career (*Spider-Man*) and
continues to inspire fledgling filmmakers the world over
through its gonzo filmmaking aesthetic.

Conceived in the spirit of slasher-stalker films like
Halloween and *Friday the 13th*, *The Evil Dead* pits a group of
teens together in a shack in the middle of the woods where
they come across The Book of the Dead, which, upon
reading, unleashes an unspeakable evil. One by one, they turn
into 'deadites' (similar to the zombie myth, but referred to as
'demons' and 'demon resurrection') in a series of now-
legendary horror sequences – think 'pencil in ankle' and 'rape
by forest'.

The word 'rape' doesn't usually coincide with fun, but *The
Evil Dead* is most certainly an exercise in thrills and spills.
Both of the film's sequels, directed by Sam Raimi, increase
the ridiculousness exponentially. It's a movie that doesn't

exist in isolation – in fact, the sequel, *Evil Dead II* (1987), is a hoot, and the second sequel, *Army of Darkness* (1992), is arguably the best of the bunch.

Devil Doll (1964)

Director: Lindsay Shonteff, UK

There was much toying – pardon the pun – with whether to include *Devil Doll* in a book on monster movies. Without spoiling the plotline, the so-called 'monster' is not so clear-cut. But as far as possessed toys go, the deeply carved 'Hugo' dummy, partner of ventriloquist The Great Vorelli – with his permanent grin, HUGE ears, synthetic hair, thickly painted eyebrows and lifeless eyes – blows the likes of Chucky out of the water.

A tense, psychological, low-budget flick, *Devil Doll* is filmed with tight foreground/background two-shots, close reveals on the actors' faces and dramatic camera angles – usually from below. The cheeky 'continental' version offers a titillating striptease and, generally, more flesh.

For more entertaining jaunts with malevolent dummies, check out the 'ventriloquist's dummy' segment from the quintet of stories, *Dead of Night* (1945, directed by Alberto Cavalcanti) and Richard Attenborough's *Magic* (1978), written by William Goldman and starring a young Anthony Hopkins.

EMMA WESTWOOD

The Omen (1976)

Director: Richard Donner, UK/USA

While not this author's favourite movie, it's hard to ignore
The Omen when mentioning films on demons. Starring Lee
Remick and Gregory Peck as the terrorised parents of an
abnormally wicked child and based on a novel by David
Seltzer, this suspense-thriller cleaned up at the box office,
produced three sequels and was remade in 2006 – not to
mention the negative publicity it generated for anyone called
'Damien'.

Given the commerciality of *The Omen*, it should be duly
noted that it contains a couple of delightfully nasty scenes –
a decapitation by a sheet of glass, which was a first for the
Hollywood system, and a hanging at a child's birthday party.
Of course, there were the rumours of a curse that plagued
the production of the film, but that goes part and parcel with
stuff of this nature (see the rest of this chapter for further
examples).

From the Desk of...
Bong Joon-ho
(South Korea)

'*Even more than the 1933 King Kong, Bong's creature is a surreal entity with no fixed size. As the materialisation of dread, this nameless monster is harder to pin down than the radioactive, fire-breathing Godzilla. It's an "It".*' – review of *The Host* by J. Hoberman, *Village Voice* (6 March 2007)

Filmography: *Barking Dogs Never Bite* (2000), *Memories of Murder* (2003), *The Host* (2006)

Personally, as a filmmaker, with *The Host*, I wanted the challenge of directing a monster/creature genre film. I think the monster/creature genre has its very own cinematic thrills and excitements. At the same time, I wanted to make a film that was unique for this genre, so the dual desire inspired me.

But I belong to the Korean film industry and, in Korea, the monster/creature genre is looked down upon in the artistic sense. As for the technical and industrial aspects, the genre film is also considered a high-risk business so, as soon as I decided to work on *The Host*, I had to stand up to the concerns and contempt of many of my fellow filmmakers. That also worked as an inspiration for me, though. I was attracted to this project because I wanted to make a monster/creature genre movie that defied its genre conventions.

I wouldn't call myself an obsessive who only watches creature/monster genre films, but it is true that I love John Carpenter's *The Thing* and Japanese horror films by Kurosawa Kiyoshi. I remember watching *Gojira* (*Godzilla*) on TV through American Forces Network when I was young. In particular, I have a strong recollection of the three-headed monster, King Ghidorah.

Though I have distinctive memories of the monsters in films I watched when I was young, I don't think *The Host* is specifically related to these movies. My creature designer, Jang Hee-chul, and myself wanted the creature to have the most genuine feelings with a very subtle orientalism. Therefore, rather than resorting to the existing monsters in films and comic books, we referred to real mutant creatures.

The creature in *The Host* – its size and action pattern in the Han River – was based on my own concepts, but I worked with my creature designer from the very beginning. I worked on the look of the monster for about a year and a half, as well as writing the scenario, so the look developed alongside the scenario as the creature needed certain features to drive the narrative.

It is the core idea of the script that the monster doesn't simply eat the victims, but carries them to a hideout. The story is a kind of kidnapping story where the bad guys are replaced by the creature. In the real animal kingdom, a pelican puts the fish in its pocket near its beak to carry its prey to babies in the nest – or a better example would be squirrels storing their food – so the monster's habit is a natural, common-sense thing.

I got the idea of the monster throwing up bones from reptiles like the anaconda. The bones you see in the film belong to the victims in the beginning – they've been digesting in the monster's stomach for a long time. Reptiles like the anaconda swallow cows and sheep much bigger than themselves then digest them over two or three weeks before they throw up the bones and start feeding again.

In the DVD of *The Host* released in Japan and Korea, there is a supplement where you see the film from the creature's point of view. You can learn things about its habits that are not explained in the film, like why it carries people and when it decides to eat them.

The monster design you see in the film is the final one, but there were lots of models that weren't chosen. Among them, there were some magnificent monster designs that might work as main characters in other creature/monster movies. There was one designer whose model wasn't chosen, so the two designers worked in a kind of competitive environment. When the design was set, the visualisation was completed by Weta Workshop (New Zealand) who were in charge of the scannable maquette. John Cox Workshop in Australia made the actual size head puppet of the monster and the computer graphics were done by the US company The Orphanage.

A fish or amphibian was the basis for the monster design in *The Host*, which means it has less personality and human-like feelings than a monster like King Kong, which is a mammal. But I tried to achieve some humanness through its behaviour patterns. It was very important to give the impression that the monster is somewhat clumsy, like when it misses its footing or rolls down the slopes when it first attacks people, so I wanted to have clumsiness alongside the violence.

I didn't want it to be like Hannibal Lecter who's full of charisma in *The Silence of the Lambs*, but more like Steve Buscemi in *Fargo*. My creature designer and I often thought about Steve Buscemi while working on the creature design – it might look dumb but it's cleverly wicked. In other words, it is a very complicated character, just like Buscemi in *Fargo*. The monster also has an unpredictable personality, like when it cruelly kills Hee-bong or when it puts Hyun-seo down when she tries to escape by jumping from its back. I didn't want the audience to anticipate what the monster would do in the next scene, so I could maintain the tension and horror using a relatively small creature without charisma.

If I had the opportunity to create this monster again, I would make it more agitated, jumping up and down and everywhere, just like a puppy that can't hold onto its pee. I wouldn't let it stay still, not even for a second.

I never expected the huge box-office success of *The Host* in Korea. When I prepared this film, all of the local film industry people and journalists and even some of the film's crew were a little negative about its prospects. It's difficult guessing why the film was so successful but, if you insist on an answer, I think it's because of the family characters – the helpless family members were something Korean audiences could sympathise with and they were played so well by five great actors.

I'm not sure how deeply Western audiences understand the Korean situations in the film, but the story is about the universal theme of family and also of weak people, so I think it works anywhere in the world. The power of the movie is in its ability to convey human emotions that transcend borderlines and ethnic groups.

I watched the film as part of the Toronto Film Festival's Midnight Madness programme, and people whistled and cheered when the creature appeared. I think they are genre obsessives, though. In Korea, not that many people are into the genre, so they sympathise more with the family characters, which is what I intended. However, even the US genre fans who first cheered for the monster when it killed people or ran around, they gradually become engrossed in the family too, so in the end the reaction ends up being the same as the reaction in Korea.

Regardless of age, sex or nationality, people want to see monsters. The more hideous and ugly the monsters are, the more people want to see them. I think it is our weird human impulse that we want to witness the most bizarre and horrible things on screen while sitting safely in the cinema. Something about the creature films touches the deepest side of the human subconscious. The reason why even a small child wants to watch creature films is not because the child is juvenile, but because the creature film has something that stimulates the purest human instinct.

I would make another monster movie, but not a sequel to *The Host* – it would have to be about a different monster and have different characters and background. Many people ask me about a remake of *The Host* – if a truly amazing remake comes out, then I will be happy as the original director. If the remake turns out to be a disastrously stupid film, then the original will be considered greater than the new one, so I don't mind that either.

The remake is solely the director of the remake's responsibility. I am now concentrating on conceiving new stories for my future projects, so I don't want to be involved in any

EMMA WESTWOOD

remake project. Of course, I think the studio has no intention to ask my participation, either! I don't mind if they create everything new and different, but, personally, I hope that the main family characters remain as loser characters, just like the original.

Daaaaaaa... dum... Daaaaaaa... dum
Monsters from the Deep

No one really knows what lies beneath the water's surface. With the aid of technology, we've seen images of nightmarish deep-sea creatures, and we've also concocted our own underwater monster myths, the likes of mermaids and mermen, and giant octopi with hankering appetites for fishermen. Next time you dip your toe in the water, spare a thought for what might be lurking below...

The Beast from 20,000 Fathoms (1953)

Director: Eugène Lourié, USA

While the 'Beast' may not be as well known as a few of its creature compadres – and has lost a modicum of shine over time – this movie occupies a very important place in cinema history: it's the first film to feature a monster that has been either awakened or created as a result of nuclear energy.

This may initially seem like a tawdry credit, but trip your mind through the many radioactive monsters that have captivated audiences over the post-World War Two decades – whether *Godzilla* (p.92) or something of a more B-movie

89

nature, like *Fiend without a Face* (p.54) – and you start to form a picture of this film's significance.

Not only that, but *The Beast from 20,000 Fathoms* had a couple of other 'firsts' to add to its honour roll: it was the first feature-length adaptation of a work by science fiction author Ray Bradbury and it was also the first film in which stop-motion mastermind Ray Harryhausen (see *The Seventh Voyage of Sinbad*, p.23, and *Jason and the Argonauts*, p.31) had complete control over his special effects. (Note: Harryhausen and Bradbury are friends and self-confessed dinosaur 'freaks'.)

After being inadvertently thawed from ice following an atomic detonation, a 100-million-year-old rhedosaurus slowly makes its way from the Arctic to New York City, terrorising some unsuspecting seamen along the way and causing many an impassioned argument over whether such a phenomenon could actually occur or not. Of course, the naysayers are forced to swallow their words when this prehis-toric mammoth finds itself in the midst of New York City, eventually attracted to the bright lights and rollercoaster rides of Coney Island where the film's exciting finale takes place.

While Harryhausen's dinosaur effects, having been honed by a valuable apprenticeship with Willis O'Brien (effects wiz on *The Lost World*, p.28), demand most of your attention, watch for the super-thrilling giant-squid-versus-shark underwater tousle that, unlike the 'Beast' himself, is the real deal. No trickery required.

Physicality: Palaeontologists may disagree, but the rhedo-saurus doesn't seem physically equipped for a life in the ocean. Where is the porpoise tail, fins or webbing? As far as this untrained eye can tell, he's just a big, thundering dinosaur who clomps along the ocean floor with a tsunami-generating intensity.

We are told, though, that he has a skull that is at least eight inches thick and, reportedly, Harryhausen built his model to scale – 50 feet.

Personality: This rhedosaurus is fairly vanilla when it comes to the personality stakes, which is probably one of the reasons why it has taken a backseat to other more alluring monsters over the course of time. But, lack of personality doesn't equate with lack of rage, as demonstrated by its terrorisation of Manhattan and the smashing up of a lighthouse as though it was made of matchsticks.

Lineage and Legacy: At one point during *The Beast from 20,000 Fathoms*, a wise character surmises, 'What the cumulative effects of all these atomic tests and explosions will be, only time can tell.'

After sitting through many a nuclear-monster flick since the film's release in 1953, it's pretty clear that atomic energy not only has the power to annihilate on a mass scale, but can generate healthy profits at the box office. *Beast* was made independently and cheaply for US$200,000, but was one of the biggest earners of that year.

For all those magnified creatures, the size and mutation of which only nuclear energy could create, we have *The Beast from 20,000 Fathoms* to thank. God bless.

EMMA WESTWOOD

Godzilla (1954)
aka *Gojira*

Director: Ishirô Honda, Japan

Having generated 28 movies over 50 years, *Godzilla* is the granddaddy of Eastern monster movies and the inspiration for a steady stream of other overblown monsters, whether allies, foes or children of the T-Rex look-alike.

While it would be apt to place Godzilla in the 'Big Monster' category, his origins are from the inky depths of the ocean — one of the few places large enough to conceal such a prehistoric monstrosity. As one of the characters in the film says, 'Godzilla... It's the name of a monster that lives in the sea. It will come from the ocean to feed on humankind to survive. In the old days, during times when the fishing was poor, we used to sacrifice girls to prevent him from eating us all, yes!'

The now famous name of 'Gojira' is a combination of 'gorilla' and the Japanese word for 'whale' — 'kujira'. Due to mispronunciation, a Western audience came to know him as 'Godzilla' and this nomenclature was the one that stuck.

Producer Tomoyuki Tanaka originally planned to make a period drama for Japan's Toho Studios, but, encouraged by the success of a re-released *King Kong* (p.14) in 1952 and *The Beast from 20,000 Fathoms* (p.89) at the Japanese box office, decided to try his hand at a monster movie. His decision proved a fruitful one. The *New York Times* labelled the original film directed by Ishirô Honda — who would go on to direct nine Godzilla films — as 'the pre-eminent monster movie of the 50s'.

Even though *Godzilla* achieved notoriety in the US, producer Joseph Levine re-edited the film with a series of inserts and a dilution of what could have been deemed as anti-American sentiments. It is important to note that the 'nuclear issue' was particularly delicate only a decade after the end of World War Two. As the palaeontologist prophetically warns, 'If we keep on conducting nuclear tests, it's possible another Godzilla might appear...'

Interestingly, Levine's version turned out to be a markedly different film, entitled *Godzilla: King of the Monsters* (1956, directed by Terry Morse) – shorter in length, and featuring the newly introduced central character of a foreign news correspondent called Steve Martin (played by Raymond Burr), who is intercut somewhat awkwardly with the original cast and dictates the action via a dense audio narration.

While both films have their merits – if for nothing more than their curiously different handling of post-atomic bomb Japan – it's the austerity of Honda's original film, unfolded with military precision and not even a skerrick of irony, that makes it a monster movie never to be forgotten. The name 'Godzilla' may make people giggle these days, but the first film is certainly nothing to laugh about.

Physicality: Weighing 20,000 metric tonnes and reaching 50 metres in height, Godzilla – a throwback to the Jurassic era of dinosaurs – careens through buildings as if they're made of clay and gnaws through train carriages like grissini sticks. The product of hydrogen bomb tests in the Pacific Ocean, he is radioactive from head to foot, a fact most impressively demonstrated by the fiery breath that can set anything on fire and melt steel into a malleable jelly.

Unlike the films that inspired *Godzilla*, Honda wanted greater fluidity to the movement of his monster, rather than the staccato effect of stop-motion animation. To do this, he enlisted two actors/stuntmen to alternate as Godzilla in a rubber suit – replete with fangs, weeny ears and four toes per foot – which proved a gruelling task as the costume was weighty and poorly ventilated.

The film's composer, Akira Ifukube, created Godzilla's roar by altering the sounds of bass fiddle strings scraped by a gloved hand.

Personality: Riding high on radioactivity, Godzilla is hostile, to say the least, but his personality mutated along with the franchise.

By the time *Ghidorah, the Three-Headed Monster* (1964) came around, Godzilla had become far more heroic. In fact, a translated conversation in that film between Godzilla and some other monsters attributes his animosity towards mankind as being caused by unprovoked attacks by humans. Poor Godzilla.

Lineage and Legacy: *Godzilla* was the first of the *Kaiju Eiga* or 'Giant Monster' movies that would colour Japanese cinema for many decades to come. Once it was obvious man was no match for this larger-than-life creature, it was necessary to introduce other monsters to fuel further battles and greater thrills.

Some monster names include Anguirus, Baragon, Battra, Biollante, Dagahra, Dagora, Destoroyah, Desghidorah, Ebirah, Gabra, Gaira, Ganima, Gezora, Gigan, Gorosaurus, Hedorah, Jet Jaguar, Kamacuras, Kameba, King Seesar,

Kumonga, Magma, Manda, King Ghidorah, Mecha-King Ghidorah, Mechagodzilla, Megaguirus, Megalon, Minilla, Moguera, Monster X, Mothra, Orga, Rodan, Sanda, Spacegodzilla, Titanosaurus, Varan and even a cyborg duplicate of King Kong called 'Mechani-Kong', and a 'reimagining' of Frankenstein, also called 'Frankenstein'.

Much bigger than the monster first portrayed in 1954, the legend of Godzilla has become an industry all of its own. To date, Godzilla has undergone eight distinctive makeovers as a character, as well as some non-Japanese versions that are largely considered non-kosher (let's not even talk about *that* American film). Godzilla's rival from the Daiei Motion Picture Company is the giant flying turtle, Gamera (p.31).

Jaws (1975)

Director: Steven Spielberg, USA

It's the film that coined the term 'blockbuster', becoming the world's highest-grossing feature for a couple of years before *Star Wars* toppled it from the mantel. Based on a best-selling novel by Peter Benchley, *Jaws* is a milestone for twentieth-century cinema, not just for monster movies.

At the time of its making, Steven Spielberg was a renegade 29-year-old director with only one theatrical release to his name, *The Sugarland Express*. Obstinate and possibly naïve, he elected to shoot *Jaws* off the coast of Martha's Vineyard, rather than on controlled sets, which proved a trial of errors on so many levels. Ships would appear on the horizon, which would delay shooting for hours on end, the crew boat sank and equipment was submerged. As the problems escalated, so did the budget – Spielberg was heading for career purgatory if this gamble didn't pay off, but, luckily for him, it did.

The stories of woe that came out of the making of *Jaws* have been documented in excellent DVD collectors' editions (one such edition was released on the 25th anniversary of the film) and make for imperative viewing for anyone vaguely interested in the mechanics of the filmmaking process.

The shark may be the monster, but this film itself is monstrous in so many ways.

Physicality: While footage of real sharks shot by Australian shark experts Ron and Valerie Taylor was incorporated into the final edit, the 'Jaws' that we all know and love – the monster that leaps out at us when we're taking the tour at Universal Studios in Hollywood – is actually a composite of three mechanical sharks, constructed by production designer Joe Alves (who earned a Golden Raspberry nomination for his first and final directorial effort, *Jaws 3-D*) and special-effects artist Bob Mattey.

One shark was used for full-body underwater shots, while the other two turned either left or right and, therefore, had exposed mechanical insides depending on which way they were designed to turn.

If this all sounds complicated, well, the wrangling of this trio of mechanical sharks *was* complicated. Often, shooting was stalled due to the sharks not functioning in the salt water – their insides corroding – or even sinking to the bottom of the ocean.

As far as filmmaking frustrations go, *Jaws* topped the list, but most will say the headaches were well worth it, even if there are punters who still persist in grumbling about the shark not looking real enough. Given the suddenness of the shark attacks, its seeming invisibility underwater and the brevity of its screen time, by the time we're given any decent look at this underwater hunter, we're totally engrossed in the adventure of it all… and any rubberiness is forgiven.

Personality: Mirroring the behaviour of a real shark, this great white is a soulless killing machine that devours with an unmerciful precision – a stealthy hunter that takes its prey unawares. Robert Shaw, as Quint, sums up its personality best in a chilling monologue describing the blackness of its eyes until they roll back white during a bite.

What makes this shark special, though, in a film-monster kind of way, is its intelligence and ability to outwit its human adversaries at almost every turn.

Lineage and Legacy: Given the cold hard cash *Jaws* raked in, a sequel (or more) was destined. Spielberg had severed his involvement with the giant shark pretty much as soon as he'd flown the Martha's Vineyard coop – apparently, he still suffers from recurring nightmares where he is back on the third day of the shoot – but the studio was keen to make good on the *Jaws* name. *Jaws 2*, *Jaws 3-D* and *Jaws: The Revenge* followed.

Where *Jaws*' greatest legacy exists, though, is its influence on filmmaking. Thirty years on, and John Williams' distinctive musical theme subconsciously announces a shark attack even out of its original context, the film frequently crops up on lists honouring the greatest films of all time and even Ridley Scott's *Alien* was pitched as 'Jaws in space'. Quite literally, the list goes on.

No matter how you'd like to intellectualise it, everything

comes down to just one thing: *Jaws* is entertainment at its best. Few movies can maintain their gloss and thrills on multiple viewings as *Jaws* does, and a monster movie at that.

Creature from the Black Lagoon (1954)

Director: Jack Arnold, USA

The last of Universal Studios' classic monster movies, *Creature from the Black Lagoon* comes from filmmaker Jack Arnold, who would be remembered as a master of 1950s sci-fi with a repertoire of *It Came from Outer Space*, *Tarantula* and *The Incredible Shrinking Man*.

Appealing to the teen market, *Creature* was originally released in 3-D, a techno gimmick at the height of its popularity at this time. More than just a date flick hinged on a fad, though, the film pushed notions of evolution as its theme, while even foreshadowing contemporary debates about environmentalism – in particular, watch for when actress Julia Adams as Kay nonchalantly tosses a cigarette in the water, followed by a scene of floating dead fish as a result of their experimentation in the lagoon.

Even though the amphibious Creature can walk (nay, shuffle) on land, the majority of his sequences take place underwater – hallucinogenic, dreamlike and suitably eerie as he glides through the reeds. Dialogue-free, they are highly choreographed, accompanied by a dense music score and a harsh horn theme (either that or Kay's screams) that heralds the Creature whenever he appears (four composers worked on this composite score, including Henry Mancini).

Creature from the Black Lagoon was a sexy re-jig for scientists, who got to break free from nerdy stereotypes. They strut around the Amazon jungle, some might say a little homo-erotically, with bare, muscled chests and super-tight swimming trunks. Kay's coy – but, for the 50s, very risqué – swimsuit was designed specifically for her, cut cheekily up the thigh. No wonder the Creature falls in love with her.

Physicality: By the time *Creature from the Black Lagoon* went into production in the 50s, Universal's legendary Head of Makeup, Jack Pierce (*Frankenstein*, p.38), had retired and Bud Westmore (the brother of Wally Westmore, who had been responsible for the makeup effects on *Dr Jekyll & Mr Hyde*, p.45) had taken up the slack. Westmore was the front man, but the lagoon's Creature was the culmination of a creative team effort, notably the glamorous Millicent Patrick whose sketches realised his final appearance.

Originally, the Creature was conceived as a more stream-lined, eel-like monster. However, his final incarnation was quite lumpy and bumpy with protruding gills, fins and scales, the gills even flexing for his close-up. It also took two actors to animate the Creature – one for above water (Ben Chapman) and one below (Ricou Browning, who had impressed Jack Arnold with his elegant swimming technique). Both men were subjected to full-body moulds from which one-piece body stockings were created and then decorated with various adornments of foam and rubber. Ten-pound weights were attached to the bottom of Chapman's shoes so that he'd shuffle when walking on land, in the manner, they guessed, of a sea-creature-cum-man. Whenever the Creature makes a noise, he sounds kind of similar to a walrus.

Marketing materials often depicted the Creature as quite

garish in bright greens and with large protruding red lips. In actuality, he was far more subtle-looking, coloured so that he could easily hide, camouflaged among the mossy reeds.

Personality: Generally pissed off – but wouldn't you be too if a group of nosey scientists decided to plunder your home? – this Creature seems hell-bent on disposing of his uninvited visitors one by one.

But he is partially man, after all, and the presence of an attractive female on the crew has him somewhat smitten à la *Beauty and the Beast*. In an emotionally and photographically moving sequence where she slips into the water for a swim, he chooses not to strike, but instead observes her water ballet and even mirrors her movements as he glides surreptitiously below her.

Cunning and smart, the Creature constantly foils the intruders by attacking them unawares and laying traps to prevent their escape. This is one smart amphibian.

Lineage and Legacy: Ushering in a new age of monster moviemaking, *Creature from the Black Lagoon* set a precedent for the likes of *Alien* (p.139) and *Predator* (p. 156). In other words, this green-slimy-man-in-a-suit was highly influential.

He also kicked off his own franchise, which led to *Revenge of the Creature* (1955, also directed by Jack Arnold) and *The Creature Walks Among Us* (1956, directed by John Sherwood). Continuing their social commentary, the first sequel was a product of the Cold War with themes of invasion and social turmoil, while the second was the heaviest in terms of pathos with the Creature becoming more like man and being clumsier and depressed because of it.

If ever the legacy of the *Creature from the Black Lagoon* was under question, this quote about him from Marilyn Monroe in *The Seven Year Itch* says it all: 'He wasn't really all bad. I think he just craved a little affection, you know. A sense of being wanted and needed.' Maybe there's a little bit of the Creature in all of us.

Deep Rising (1998)

Director: Stephen Sommers, USA

Coming from the directorial command and scripting pen of Stephen Sommers (1999's *The Mummy* and *Van Helsing* – but don't hold those gobblers against him), *Deep Rising* is one insane hootenanny of a good time. If you're not ready for it, then the triumphant battle cry of the opening title music will prep you for the onslaught to come.

There's nothing slow about *Deep Rising* and nothing particularly deep, despite the use of such a word in the title. The focus here is on Schwarzenegger-style action over horror, although spiced with some tasty treats like 'half-digested Billy', who has an entire special-effects team credited to him.

The movie follows the maiden voyage of a luxury ocean liner (read: instant disaster ever since the *Titanic*), fitted to the gills with exorbitantly rich so-and-sos hopped up on champagne, who are about to suffer a rude awakening. When a rag-tag team of mercenaries led by Treat Williams storms the unnervingly quiet ship, they find it deserted, except for a woman dressed in red (Famke Janssen), locked in the cold storage. Very quickly, the plot thickens as some computer-generated, worm-like tentacles attack the ship's gatecrashers.

Nowhere is safe, even when taking a seat on the crapper.

To flesh out the fun and games, there is a nutty sidekick, a token dry Aussie, a sleazy ship owner of dubious intention and a nice muzak version of *The Girl from Ipanema*. If that equation doesn't add up to 'woo hoo', then what the hell does?

Physicality: At one point, the hijackers speculate that these giant worms, which can scoot rapidly down corridors (and even roar!), are members of the Ottoia family – a type of deep-sea worm – that has somehow ballooned to an immeasurable size while hiding in ocean trenches.

Apparently, at 20,000 feet, the Ottoia have been known to eat full-grown sharks so, on that basis, the deeper they get, the more monstrous they become. The crafty Ottoia have spines along their length that scientists believe to be teeth for capturing their prey. In this movie, they are not so interested in munching on their victims as drinking them while they're still alive – sucking out every morsel of nourishment before spitting out the bones like picked-over chicken carcasses.

As one of the gung-ho hijackers so delicately puts it, though: 'Who gives a shit what they are? Just tell us how to kill these motherfuckers.'

Personality: It's not a stretch to say that worms aren't celebrated for their personality, but there is something definitely different about these worms – their omnipresence, their intelligence, their ability to work as a seemingly cohesive force… hmmmmmm…

Lineage and Legacy: It's doubtful any filmmakers are repeatedly watching *Deep Rising*, exploring its ins and outs to inform their own movies, although many may be guiltily indulging in Saturday-night sessions just for the fun of it. Sommers, however, pays his respects to the likes of *Jason and the Argonauts* (p.31, supposedly one of his favourite movies) by naming the film's cruise liner *Argonautica* – tagline: 'your fun ship!'

There's something about the watery tentacles reaching inside the nooks and crannies of the ship that may remind one of James Cameron's *The Abyss*, although that's where any similarities abruptly end. *Deep Rising* is as serious as a paper cut.

And Then Some...

Rogue (2007)

Director: Greg McLean, Australia

Once again using the dwarfing isolation of Australia's outback as his stage, filmmaker Greg McLean (*Wolf Creek*) sends some unsuspecting tourists down a river system in the Northern Territory and, in the simplest of tried-and-tested storylines, picks them off one by one.

McLean drew from the talents of the Weta Workshop crew to make his rogue croc as realistic as possible, with definite nods to the likes of *Jaws* (p.95). Just as Spielberg's shark uses the sea as its cloak for a surprise attack, *Rogue's* prehistoric beast is only seen when it wants to be seen. The crocodile's actual instincts are exacted to the full extent, right down to the victim 'death roll', its nesting habits and territorial persuasions.

Rogue might not dive into the emotional depths of its

characters like *Jaws* (p.95) does, but it masterfully establishes a quirky ensemble with unique foibles and personality traits that makes predicting who will die and who will
survive all the more challenging. A rollicking good date
film.

Piranha II: The Spawning (1981)

Director: James Cameron, USA

Many people would dispute the inclusion of this Italo-
American sequel to a cheesy *Jaws* rip-off in a chronicle of
quality monster cinema. The film is certainly corny – yes –
but there's something endearing about this first feature by
Titanic director James Cameron.

It's said executive producer Ovidio G. Assonitis wrenched
directorial control from Cameron, but still it's hard to ignore
how a toothy piranha popping out of a cadaver foreshadows
one of Cameron's later films, *Aliens* (as well as the inclusion
of the po-faced Lance Henriksen in the cast). Even Cameron
admits, 'I believe *The Spawning* was the finest flying piranha
movie ever made.'

No one could dispute such a truth.

Anaconda (1997)

Director: Luis Llosa, USA/Brazil/Peru

Long before J-Lo's 'shelf booty' became famous and
they employed a stylist to give her the Hollywood
re-jig, she starred in this absolute hoot-fest of a flick that is rife

with blatant phallic symbols and riotous attack sequences.

Accompanied by Ice Cube and Eric Stoltz in the supporting cast, Jennifer Lopez plays a filmmaker for *National Geographic*, drifting down the Amazon tributaries on her mission to shoot a documentary on a lost Indian tribe. An eccentric snake hunter, played with scene-stealing levels of cheese by Jon Voigt, seconds the film crew's field trip. While he presents himself under the ruse of being able to locate the tribe, he has an ulterior motive: to capture the world's largest anaconda, which, in this case, is extremely big, ridiculous and cheaply computer-generated.

Anaconda is the kind of film that critics hate because it is dumb with a capital 'D' – but they're taking their job a little too seriously. Pay attention to Jon Voigt and you'll soon be in on the joke and, consequently, enjoying the ride along with him.

Attack of the Crab Monsters (1957)

Director: Roger Corman, USA

Roger Corman's mantle as king of the B-monsters is firmly established here with the beguiling yet utterly ridiculous *Attack of the Crab Monsters*, which originally screened as a double bill with *Not of this Earth* (p.155).

A genius of marketing and maths rather than 'serious' film-making, Corman attracted an audience for his film as much through the title as the content. But as far as plotlines go – and this one has many holes to fall through – it sees a group of scientists converge on an island to research the effects of nuclear tests. When they arrive, they discover a strain of massive crustaceans that have already killed off the previous research expedition and absorbed their brains as an intellect booster.

The monsters may enjoy brains, but everything else about this film is pretty much a no-brainer – and not surprisingly considering it is one of ten features that Corman directed in 1957 alone. Cheap and nasty fun.

It Came from Beneath the Sea (1955)

Director: Robert Gordon, USA

This time, Ray Harryhausen's stop-motion effects go underwater in the form of a giant octopus that wrestles with scientists and nuclear submarines before taking down San Francisco's Golden Gate Bridge. This tangled mutation hails from the Mindanao Deep region of the ocean, but appears to have been unceremoniously dislodged by hydrogen bomb tests in the area.

Quite obviously an attempt to capitalise on the success of its atomic predecessor, *The Beast from 20,000 Fathoms* (p.89), *It Came from Beneath the Sea* was made on the smell of an oily rag and, possibly, at an accelerated speed, which could excuse any of its failings as a film. The budget couldn't even cover the eight-tentacle requirement to make the monster anatomically correct, so Harryhausen animated six tentacles instead, dubbing his disabled creature 'the sextapus'.

Whatever you think of *It Came from Beneath the Sea* in terms of storyline and dramatic conflict, it contains a Harryhausen monster and, for fans of such marvellous oddities, that's enough reason to waste the 79 minutes it will take you to watch this film.

From the Desk of...
Ryuhei Kitamura
(Japan)

'Holy cow! It's a giant monster movie! No, wait... it's an alien inva-sion movie! No, it's actually a martial-arts movie! Wait... it might actually be all three!' – review of *Godzilla: Final Wars* by Moriarty, aintitcool.com (30 November 2004)

Filmography: *Versus* (2000), *Alive* (2002), *Aragami* (2003), *Azumi* (2003), *Sky High* (2003), *Godzilla: Final Wars* (*Gojira: Fainaru uôzu*, 2004), *LoveDeath* (2006), *Midnight Meat Train* (2008)

Of course, being Japanese, I grew up watching Godzilla movies. I was a fan of the original movie and the ones from the 70s – that's when Godzilla movies were really crazy. My favourite is *Godzilla vs. Mechagodzilla* (*Gojira tai Mekagojira*, 1974). I don't even remember the first time that I saw it, but that movie was full of fun – it's very creative, full of passion, not very serious at all.

The original *Godzilla* (*Gojira*, 1954) is a very special movie. It's something very different. It has a strong message against war, against nuclear arms... At the time, the original creator (Ishirô Honda) probably had to do a film that was like that. But then they made 26 movies after the original, and 50 years is a long history of Godzilla, and they just keep on doing the same thing.

I wasn't a big fan of Godzilla movies after the 80s. That's when I stopped watching them. The name 'Godzilla' is a huge title in Japan. It has fans all over the world, lots of history. But Godzilla became too huge and I felt that, after the 80s, the creators took it too seriously. They were afraid to challenge with something new and just kept doing same thing, same way. Why do the Japanese Self-Defence Forces always have to fight against Godzilla? There's no room for fun.

Godzilla is science fiction. If you care about the reality, when a big monster comes out and attacks Tokyo, Osaka, or whatever city in Japan, of course the self-defence force will fight against it, because that's the only army in Japan, right? But I feel, come on, forget the reality – it's fun, it's entertainment. There will never be Godzilla in our real world. Maybe a creature like what's in *The Host*, but never Godzilla. But many Japanese filmmakers want to make films with too much reality and that's what makes movies boring. I believe that movies should be something that takes you out of reality.

If you have to shoot the self-defence force, then you have to go to the self-defence force for their cooperation. Then, there are lots and lots and lots of rules. You get notes from them saying, 'No, we don't like this, we don't like that.' I lost interest when I saw things like that happening in Godzilla movies in the 80s. They just kept on doing the same thing – like the 70s, but with less quality. That's what I felt, anyway. Because of the size of the title, Godzilla just went too big and too conservative.

When the producer asked me to do *Godzilla: Final Wars*, I tried to be honest right from the start. I wanted to be in synch with him, otherwise it would be a mess. So the first thing I said was, 'Wow, why me?' The producer came to me three days after the release of my movie *Azumi*. That was my first big studio movie in Japan and it was one of the biggest movies in Japan for 2003. I was a strange type of director in Japan. I was always independent and never was a part of a studio or production company. Until *Versus* came out, I was nobody and just 32 years old.

I told the producer of the Godzilla films that I was a big fan of the movies back in the 70s but, to be honest, after the 80s, Godzilla movies hadn't been good. I told him that I didn't even go to see Godzilla movies any more – 'You guys keep on doing the same thing, but only for the kids or Godzilla freaks. I can't call my girlfriend and say, "Come on, let's go and check out the new Godzilla movie." It's never going to happen. It's obvious you're losing your audience and it's a dying franchise.'

I told him exactly this and he said, 'I know and we know.' He said that it was the 50th anniversary and they'd decided to finish the Godzilla series. For how long, he wasn't sure, but he had to finish it right now. This producer, Mr Tomiyama – he's the one who revived Godzilla in the 80s and he's the one who's been doing Godzilla for the past 15 years. That's why I told him that I didn't like what he was doing. And he understood that. For the final Godzilla, he wanted to do something new.

Mr Tomiyama told me he was so impressed with what I did – that I reinvigorated the Japanese action movie with *Azumi* – so he believed I could do something new with

Godzilla. I said, 'Oh, OK.' But I told him, 'If you want me to do the same thing that you've been doing for the last 10 or 15 years, I don't think I'm the one – you can find someone else. You think you can fool kids by doing the same thing again and again and again. Nowadays, kids have much more sense than we do. They go to see *Lord of the Rings*, *The Matrix*, those great movies. Why you keep doing the same old way of moviemaking? Of course you've lost your audience.'

I told him that what I wanted to make was Godzilla for *The Matrix* and *The Lord of the Rings* audience. Not the old kind of Godzilla movie. Of course, I grew up watching Godzilla movies and I do respect the title. If a director respects the project too much, though – loves it too much – and is afraid of changing, that's why Godzilla has never been updated until now. I said: 'What I'm going to do is update it. I'm going to break all the style you've been doing for the last 15 or 20 years and I'm going to do something like back in the 70s when there were no rules. If you let me do that, then I think I'm the one.' And Mr Tomiyama said, 'That's what I want to do and only you can do that.'

Some people in the film industry and some of my friends were very negative about me making a Godzilla movie, because I was an upcoming director and they saw Godzilla as dying. They said, even if you make a good movie, there won't be the audience. It was true and I understood that. But you know, as a Japanese director, Godzilla is a very special title… and the 50th anniversary… and the final Godzilla title… How could I refuse it, really?

After I was attached as a director, I told everyone that I was going to do a man in a rubber suit, the old-fashioned way. I wasn't going to use a CGI Godzilla – that's what Hollywood can do. What's good about Godzilla is it's a man in a suit. Doesn't matter that it doesn't look real. I'm sure that when they do Godzilla movies – maybe in 10 years or 15 years – I'm sure someone will do it CGI. But the man in a suit is a kind of a tradition, from the golden age of Japanese movies.

The old studio at Toho – that's where I shot the final scene where Godzilla walks into the ocean – they pulled it down after I shot there. That's where they shot a lot of legendary movies back in the 60s and 70s, but now it's no more. I wanted to catch the best of the best – the golden age of Japanese movies. I knew it was going to be the last. But, at the same time, I knew that if I thought too much like that, everything like in the 60s and 70s, then nothing would be new, right? So I said, just men in suits for all the monsters, but, for the effects, we'll use CGI and we're going to add more insane action.

The next thing I said was, 'No more self-defence force. Come on, it doesn't look cool! US Army, US Navy, US Air Force... They look cool. Look at the Japanese Self-Defence Force... It just doesn't look cool. And that's the biggest mistake you guys have been making for 20 years.' So I decided to make a totally science fiction army. That was a huge change.

The third thing I told them was I wanted to do the bleach bypass process for the look of my film. It's a way of processing the film. It got famous after the movie *Se7en*. You know, more contrast... looks cool. It's nothing special in Hollywood or even in Korea but in Japan, it costs a lot of money, so you often can't do it in Japan. But then again, back in the 60s and 70s it was nothing special, but nowadays they don't do it. Same with the screen size – I shot it in 2.35:1, which is

widescreen. Again, that costs a lot of money, so Japanese
movies don't do that either. It's super-tough to make movies
in Japan.

For *Godzilla: Final Wars*, the producer had been working
with a writer, so they had a concept. He told me that, this
time, we're going to fight all over the world and we're going
to deal with old-style monsters. I thought, 'OK, if that's what
you want, let's do that.' I warned my producer at the start,
though – 'Are you sure? Because it's going to cost lots of
money if we have to shoot all over the world.' But he said,
'It's the 50th anniversary; let's fight all over the world.' So I
said, 'OK.' The first thing I wanted to do was destroy my
second hometown: Sydney. Only in the world of Godzilla is
it an honour to be destroyed by Godzilla. That was fun. That
was my first day of shooting.

There are monsters that you must bring back. It was very
tough because we had so much history and you can never
satisfy all the fans. Everyone has their favourite monster. We
– me, the screenwriter and the producer – had all the
monster figures all over the table for our meeting. Should we
go with this? No, this. We had a big meeting, but it was a fair
one.

My favourite monsters are King Seesar, who first appeared
in *Godzilla vs. Mechagodzilla*, and Hedorah, the swamp
monster from *Godzilla vs. Hedorah* (*Gojira tai Hedorâ*, 1971),
but I didn't push anything. My favourite scene is when
soldiers fight with the big shrimp monster – the real human-
versus-big-monster scene. That's the one I think nobody had
done before. I'm very proud of that scene. That scene is
totally different for the Japanese filmmaking system.
Everyone said it was impossible to do – lots of explosions,

insane action, too dangerous. How can we do it? I said, 'We're going to do it.'

I don't think the Hollywood Godzilla movie has been accepted well – not just with Japanese audiences, but also worldwide. I like the movie, but only if it's not Godzilla. If it's just a big-lizard monster movie, then it's good. Even though I can't accept that movie as a Godzilla movie, I still prefer it 100 times more than the Godzilla movies in Japan after the 80s. That's how much I hate the recent Godzilla movies in Japan. I'm always saying this, so that's why I have many enemies in the Japanese film industry. But they look like student movies. At least the American movie has good production values.

When it comes to other monster movies, I like the *Alien* movies. It's always fun to see them. I'm very impressed by *The Host* too. It's a great movie.

I've Got Protection from Your Infection…
Monsters Spreading the Monster Disease

More insidious than the plague – and with symptoms ranging from hirsutism to immortality – 'monsterdom' can be as contagious as watching the movies themselves. They bite. They suck. They fornicate. They scratch. They'll have you turning into one of them. These are monsters of the infectious kind.

Nosferatu, eine Symphonie des Grauens (1922)

Director: F.W. Murnau, Germany (silent)

With *Nosferatu*, Murnau gave us the first cinematic imagining of the Dracula character as conceived by Bram Stoker, which should have been cause for celebration, except for one thing – he neglected to secure the permission of Stoker's widow.

Even though Max Schreck wore the nomenclature of 'Count Orlok' rather than 'Dracula', the location was changed from Transylvania to Bremen and other creative liberties taken, the film's producers weren't fooling anyone and they found themselves at the mercy of a British judge who ordered all copies of the film to be destroyed.

Luckily for us, that order was not enforceable in Germany, because no greater cinematic sacrilege could be imagined than having *Nosferatu* lost forever.

Exuding an ominous atmosphere right from the start – real-estate agent Hutter gives his beloved a gift of dead flowers – *Nosferatu* is set around the time of the Black Death, where the victims of vampirism could be confused with victims of the plague. As would be familiar to fans of the Stoker tale, Hutter travels to the Carpathian Mountains to discuss a real-estate venture with Orlok, where he suffers a couple of nasty 'mosquito bites' to the neck and inadvertently brings the nefarious Orlok back home with him.

Lugosi may have provided the most iconographic face for Dracula, but Schreck provided the one that would haunt our collective nightmare for generations to come. Regardless of the film's age or that it comes from cinema's silent era, the spooky imagery – like a hump-backed shadow moving up the staircase – retains its potent sense of horror even a century after the film's original release.

As the opening title card says, 'Nosferatu – does not this word sound like the call of the death bird at midnight? Take care you never utter it, lest life's pictures fade into pale shadows and ghostly dreams rise from your heart and feed on your blood.'

Physicality: Max Schreck's performance as Orlok is one of those wonders of cinematic history that never actually leaves you.

Looking distinctly like a human-sized rodent with bald head, bushy eyebrows, pointy ears and stark white talons of fingers, his interpretation of vampirism is irksome – it really makes the skin crawl – rather than being of a seductive and charismatic nature. Given the opportunity, most people would cross the road rather than cross paths with Orlok.

Usually, the ravenous bloodsucker opens his/her mouth to reveal sharpened incisors when going in for the kill. Instead, Orlok's two front teeth are long and pointy, like those of a rabbit, with which he can draw the 'hellish elixir of life'.

Personality: These days, the vampire's reputation precedes him – we just know they're not nice – and Orlok doesn't even have the conversation skills to secure him a dinner party invitation. He's mean and he wants to suck you dry. Yum, yum.

Lineage and Legacy: The influence of *Nosferatu* has been an insidious one with references to the film littering our popular culture over the last century – everything from characters in television's *Buffy the Vampire Slayer* to gothic rock bands.

In 1979, Werner Herzog attempted a stylised remake of the film with Klaus Kinski filling the Schreck role, which proved to be an excellent effort.

Willem Dafoe donned a bald cap to play the role of Max Schreck in *Shadow of the Vampire* (2000), a fictional provocation on the making of *Nosferatu*, which posits that Schreck's performance was so effective because he was actually a real vampire.

Day of the Dead (1985)

Director: George A. Romero, USA

This is the third movie in George A. Romero's seminal zombie trilogy that includes his groundbreaking comment on racism, *Night of the Living Dead* (1968) and an often-amusing dig at consumerism, *Dawn of the Dead* (1978). Before anyone protests, yes, there are another two films in the 'dead' series that were released later – *Land of the Dead* (2005) and *Diary of the Dead* (2007) – but, for all intents and purposes, the first three sit as the perfect trilogy and, therefore, should be regarded in a league of their own.

A treatise would be necessary to do justice to Romero's films but, considering space limitations in this book, take it from a bonafide fan: an investigation into monster movies wouldn't be complete without seeing these three films. Witty, insightful and unashamedly bloodthirsty, Romero pushed into uncharted territory with his exploration of the undead and, thanks to some impressive special effects by gore wiz Tom Savini, gave a serious face to a sub-genre of films that could be easily dismissed as schlock and nothing else. In Romero's hands, this couldn't be further from the truth.

One of the idiosyncrasies of Romero's zombies is that they all have their own unique personalities. Savini and his crew took the time to create a zombie army where, in the flash of a few frames, we can ascertain so much about the personalities of these slow-moving, brain-numb beings. In *Day of the Dead*, among the zombie throng, you can pick out a clown and a bride zombie, which leads to many questions about their deaths and subsequent reanimation. While they might only shuffle, they certainly pack some power behind a bite when ripping some guy's throat out.

Day of the Dead was chosen for the purposes of dissection in this book because it is the one movie from the three that offers a clearly defined zombie character. He's called 'Bub' and he's not such a bad fellow, really. Read on…

Physicality: Like all zombies, Bub is a lumbering knuckle-head with a faraway look. He's also unfortunately caught in the middle of an implosive situation where the army wants to annihilate the zombies and scientists want to study them (note: Romero's films tend to focus less on the threat of the zombies and more on the conflict between people).

Bub is the pet project of the enclave's resident 'Frankenstein' (Dr Logan), a scientific experiment to prove that zombies can be tamed and, therefore, controlled. In a former life, it looks like Bub could have been a middle-aged guy with receding hairline and a nuclear family, although we're not privy to such personal information.

As a zombie, he's a big guy whose skin has taken on a greyish-green hue, jaw and teeth have been knocked askew and clothes are soiled and a little ratty.

Personality: While it's tenuous to say that zombies have loyalties, Bub definitely becomes attached to Dr Logan on some kind of primordial level. As Dr Logan explains, the brain has been revitalised, but nothing else – these creatures, which they avoid calling 'zombies' throughout the film, operate on instinct alone.

As Bub learns simple things, he is given rewards, just like training a dog, but rewards in the form of guts and innards.

The person offering him the rewards and praise is the person he begins to regard with affection and – *voilà* – a grunting and groaning Bub turns into a thinking and feeling reanimated being.

Lineage and Legacy: The zombie is the *monster du decade* of the noughties, which has reinvigorated interest in Romero's interpretation of the genre (see *28 Days Later*, p.125). Not only have films seriously tackled the zombie phenomenon, there have been successful comedy spin-offs, most notably the hilarious 'rom-zom-com' *Shaun of the Dead* (2004), which pays its respects to Romero and Savini's creativity in so many ways (e.g. just like in *Day of the Dead*, one of the characters gets spectacularly drawn and quartered by an encroaching zombie herd).

While most 'reinterpretations' of classic films are sub-standard, especially when wrangling with masterstrokes like Romero's work, kudos must be given to Zack Snyder's remake of *Dawn of the Dead* (2004), which can stand proudly as an excellent and genuinely thrilling film in its own right. Not only does this first-time director manage to honour Romero's legacy, he injects new life into his forerunner's vision (e.g. his zombies move quickly – *really* quickly – which gives his film more pace for the MTV generation). The *Dawn of the Dead* remake also avoids falling into the trap of the 'Hollywood ending', remaining brutally bleak, even well past the final credits. Unfortunately, the remake of *Day of the Dead* lacked such shine.

With zombie films going great guns at the box office, there's probably still more life in these walking dead.

Ginger Snaps (2000)

Director: John Fawcett, Canada

Precluding the corny title, *Ginger Snaps* is a slick piece of modern gothic focusing on the Fitzgerald sisters – Ginger and Brigitte – two inseparable siblings suffering from an overdose of teenage existential angst and a morbidity that sees them constantly videotaping enactments of their own grisly deaths.

While the girls battle to differentiate themselves from the high-school throng, some things are inevitable – like menstruation. For Ginger, a sore lower back soon reveals itself as 'the curse', which she begrudgingly accepts as it runs down her legs when out walking late one night. She also attracts the attention of a not-so-friendly neighbourhood lycanthrope (i.e. someone who has been turned into a were-wolf) that has been feasting on local canines. In a spectacularly aggressive attack sequence, Ginger is savagely mauled by the lycanthrope and her wounds miraculously heal within minutes, much to both girls' amazement.

Pubescent adolescents have been known to become sexually voracious, suddenly sprout coarse hair in unusual places and adopt a bad attitude, but never have these symptoms been so pronounced… or included growing a tail. In no time, Ginger's blood fantasies turn into a real-life blood lust, which Brigitte, in an effort to hold on to her beloved sister, mops up while investigating a secret potion that could resuscitate the normally maladjusted girl she once knew.

Physicality: At face value, the monster of *Ginger Snaps* is a human–cum–beast that prowls usually banal suburbs under the eerie glow of the full moon. But, in actual fact, the real monster here is puberty, as represented by the arrival of Ginger's monthly rags. The manifestation of the werewolf is merely a thinly veiled metaphor.

As Ginger alters, her teeth become pointed, her hair changes colour (in fact, it turns prematurely white) and grows all over her body faster than she can shave it off, and her eyes start to take on a cold, milky hue. She is a changed woman.

It's not until the finale that she reaches her full maturity and, while wolf-like (on a large scale), she is covered with ghostly pale flesh and only a smattering of hair. In one of the film's opening scenes, a clip from a television show asks, 'Can this happen to a normal woman?' Well, can it? Or, more pointedly, does it?

Personality: This monster is moody, horny, irrational and ready to bite the head off any bastard that gets in her way. It might be difficult for many of the male members of the audience to understand her, but they've all been on the receiving end of her rage, possibly once a month depending on her lunar cycle.

Ginger's transformation is a dramatic one, but it's telling of the confusion, physical and emotional pain, and drama that any young woman experiences. Filmmaker John Fawcett (with a little female perspective in the writing department from Karen Walton) has put a powerful face on menstruation. She's difficult to sympathise with, because she's unlike the person she used to be, but she's in there… somewhere.

One of Ginger's most humorous, yet truthful, lines is when

she stands in the supermarket aisle with Brigitte staring at shelves of female sanitary products: 'Just so you know, the words "just" and "cramps", they don't go together.' Hallelujah, sister.

Lineage and Legacy: *Ginger Snaps* comes from the *Buffy the Vampire Slayer* school of filmmaking (also remember Michael Lehmann's *Heathers*?) where the dialogue is attitudinally snappy, every family is dysfunctional and pop-cultural references abound.

Despite being a little film with a micro budget, it produced two sequels shot back-to-back – the OK, but ultimately forgettable, *Ginger Snaps 2* (or *Ginger Snaps: Unleashed*) and *Ginger Snaps 3* (or *Ginger Snaps Back: The Beginning*, which curiously involved time travel – yikes!). Both sequels were helmed by different directors (with John Fawcett sitting in the executive producer chair) and never rose to the standards set by the first film.

If you'd like to continue camping it up with werewolf movies, try the woefully good *I Was a Teenage Werewolf* (1957), which gave Michael Landon his first starring role and a generation of juvenile delinquents something to smile about.

Daughters of Darkness (1971)
aka *Les Lèvres rouges*

Director: Harry Kümel, Belgium/France/West Germany

There's something about vampirism that lends itself to a European sensibility. Well, Count Dracula did, apparently, come from Transylvania; but that aside, the intrinsic sensuality of the vampire culture fits snugly with Europeans' general 'appreciation' of sexuality and lack of inhibition when it comes to luxuriating in the pleasures of the flesh.

When writer–director Harry Kümel set about producing the heady *Daughters of Darkness*, his objective was to create a 'chic' vampire film, steeped in pronounced stylisation and sporting a cast of beautiful young things with soft, nubile bodies that looked good in the film's many nude scenes. Heading that cast was acclaimed French actress Delphine Seyrig who, as the Countess Elizabeth Bathory – the primary 'Daughter of Darkness' – retains her dignity in high-neck gowns. Her lush and lascivious performance is central to the film and something that sets the tone from start to finish.

Inspired by the true story of a sixteenth-century Hungarian countess, *Daughters of Darkness* sees two newly-weds arrive at a deserted, but palatial, hotel in seaside Ostende in Belgium. Naïve and madly in love, their relation-ship may be passionate, but precariously bound. The chinks in their metaphorical armour are exposed when an intriguing woman and her beautiful travelling companion arrive at the hotel and lure the young couple into their fold.

The real Elizabeth Bathory is one of the most infamous serial killers in Hungarian and Slovak history, accused of torturing and killing dozens of female victims, hence the undertones of lesbianism that Kümel builds into his film. Part of her ritual involved the biting of flesh and also bathing in her victims' blood, which draws parallels with vampirism. As well as *Daughters of Darkness*, the 1971 Hammer horror film *Countess Dracula* utilised Elizabeth Bathory as its protagonist.

Daughters of Darkness moves at a languorous pace and is overwhelming '70s Europe' in its feel, which may not suit some viewers, but is intrinsically what this movie is all about. Overt symbolism decorates every scene and the wardrobe revolves around a palette of red, white and black. Seyrig and the small cast are lit like Hollywood-heyday icons in the softest of focus or with star filters – particularly nice when Seyrig wears a highly reflective mirrored gown. This is gorgeous, sumptuous stuff.

Physicality: In preparing for her role, Delphine Seyrig took her cues from Marlene Dietrich's performance in *Angel*, which gives her the persona of a glamorous star from a bygone age. Even her clothing – or 'gowns' would be a more appropriate word – recalls a long-lost era. She is elegance personified, with platinum-blonde hair in 30s Marcel waves, blood-red lips and a perpetual smile that never flickers from her lips.

When she speaks, it is with a low, husky tone and the most interesting vocal phrasing – pauses where you least expect them. She is the fulcrum of every social occasion, styled in both manner and dress in a way that means your eyes never leave her – the perfect seductress, the perfect vampire.

Personality: She may be one of the loveliest-looking monsters on celluloid, but, like her other vampire cronies, she has only one thing on her mind. And that's not making friends.

As pleasant as she may appear – tactile and intent on making new friends – it is with an ulterior motive. The countess is enraptured by beauty and, as soon as she sees the stunning Valerie, she is single-mindedly committed to completely consuming her in mind, body and spirit. Judging by her companion Ilona's compulsion to flee and to plead for death over life, we can only presume that an existence beholden to the powerful countess is akin to an existence in hell.

Lineage and Legacy: No sequels, no imitators. *Daughters of Darkness* is very much a product of its time. From the opening title sequence, there is little doubt as to what decade the film was made in and where. Despite its success, this mesmerising vampire movie has been relegated to art-house and grind-house cinemas, never making the crossover to the mainstream.

28 Days Later (2002)

Director: Danny Boyle, UK

A commentary on humankind's vulnerability to infectious diseases or 'invisible threats', *28 Days Later* acts as a chilling wake-up call at a time when reports of biological warfare, mad cow disease, SARS and bird flu litter the news.

In this case, scientists experiment on chimps to find an inhibitor, not for any particular ailment, but for the basic emotion of rage. When animal liberationists attempt to free these laboratory primates, they inadvertently unleash a highly contagious infection based on fury that brings Britain to its knees within 28 days – hence the title.

A man waking from a coma walks the deserted streets of London in scenes that have made the film famous – normally bustling areas around iconic landmarks were cordoned off for short periods of time, which the filmmakers (cinematographer Anthony Dod Mantle) then shot almost guerrilla-style using the versatile medium of digital video. Limited by time and budget, Danny Boyle and his cronies depicted a post-apocalyptic Britain never before seen and unlikely to be replicated again.

Boyle says utilising digital equipment helped contribute to the urbanscape, creating the impression of a world being viewed through surveillance cameras. He believes the film is 'a warning for us, as well as entertainment'.

There are obvious plot points and references to Romero's *Dead* trilogy here – all three films in one, right down to the 'domesticated' creature from *Day of the Dead* – but classifying *28 Days Later* as a zombie film is drawing a long bow.

Often tagged as a zombie movie, though – probably as a marketing ploy to capitalise on the recent craze for all things 'zombified' – Boyle's 'infected' contract the disease without needing to be dead first – just a drop of blood in the eye is enough to turn a rational-thinking, able-bodied person into a blood-spitting creature. Not only that, but these monsters possess human physical frailties, whereas a zombie will continue to walk unless suffering a well-aimed blow to the brain.

Physicality: Since the disease uses the host's body as its weapon, there are no pronounced physical changes, except for seriously blood-blown eyes and a propensity to cough and splutter – often haemorrhaging bucket-loads of blood from the mouth – as well as some violent twisting and jerking of the limbs.

What is also alarming about these infected beings is their speed (shot on the 'sports mode' setting of the video camera).

Propelled on human legs, they still manage to gain quite a momentum and are more likely to run you down rather than devise tactics to sneak up on you.

Personality: Considering the disease is a psychological virus – basically, rage encapsulated – this pretty much defines the personality of these creatures. They're really angry and the way to express this anger is by chomping clear through someone's flesh.

Even rats run away from them.

Lineage and Legacy: A sequel called *28 Weeks Later* was released in 2007 and proved a nifty follow-up, although Danny Boyle shifted to the executive producer chair, making room for Juan Carlos Fresnadillo as director. Boyle has already announced plans for a third film called... wait for it... *28 Months Later*.

In terms of influence, *28 Weeks Later* has resonated in the minds of its audience, enough to inspire a string of parodies – like the comedy short *48 Hours Later*, a Malaysian comedy spoof in which the events are relocated to Kuala Lumpur, *28 Hours Later*, and yet another film called *28 Seconds Later*, where a montage of events happen between 28-second pauses.

In the film *Shaun of the Dead* (2004), you'll hear a television broadcaster say: '...initial reports that the virus was caused by rage-infected monkeys have now been dismissed as complete bullshit.'

And Then Some...

Dracula (1931)

Director: Tod Browning, USA

The first talking supernatural thriller, Universal Studios' *Dracula* set the precedent for horror iconography as we know it today – huge cobwebs, long capes, spiralling staircases and vampire bats, among other accoutrements.

And not forgetting the man who would shoulder the identity of Dracula to the grave: the thick-accented Hungarian actor Béla Lugosi. His gestures and phrasing created the template from which all play-acting and vampire spoofs for generations to come would derive, and one which, for those brought up on its mimicry, is a scene-stealing performance of high camp.

Interestingly, while Tod Browning was shooting *Dracula* for Universal, they were simultaneously filming a Spanish-language version of the script using a different director (George Melford) and different actors, but on the same sets. Reportedly, once the Browning crew had wrapped for the day, the Spanish entourage would watch Browning's 'dailies' and use them as a benchmark upon which to improve.

In terms of optical effects and camerawork, the Spanish version is the more sophisticated – you could call it the Dracula equivalent of 'Beta versus VHS' – however, Carlos Villar's performance as Dracula never toppled Lugosi from his mantel.

Horror of Dracula (1958)

Director: Terence Fisher, UK

Among many aficionados, *Horror of Dracula*, produced by Britain's famed Hammer Studios, rates a high honourable mention in the stable of films dedicated to the king of the bloodsuckers. With this film, Hammer was once again piggy-backing on Universal's success, having enjoyed the spoils of Frankenstein with *The Curse of Frankenstein* (1957, also directed by Terence Fisher).

This first foray from Hammer into vampiric legend stars the charismatic Christopher Lee as the Count and Peter Cushing as his hunter, Van Helsing. Lee would identify himself with the character of Dracula as faithfully as Béla Lugosi, playing the role for Hammer a total of seven times. As an adjunct to his work with Hammer, though, he popped up in prolific Spanish horrormeister Jess Franco's *Count Dracula* (1970).

On sets lit like a theatrical stage and with blood the colour of brilliant red, *Horror of Dracula* refuses to hide its vampire in the dark or shadows, but makes the most of the shooting stock's Technicolor brightness. As the black-caped Dracula, Lee is afforded far less screen time and dialogue than Lugosi, but appears unrestrained among a cast boot-strapped into proper English politeness.

The Wolf Man (1941)

Director: George Waggner, USA

Another mainstay from the Universal horror stable, *The Wolf Man* was originally intended for Boris Karloff, but saw Lon Chaney Jr tackle the titular role. He would become the only actor to play a classic Universal monster over a full series of five films.

Claude Rains as the Wolf Man's father delivers the prophetic definition of lycanthropy: 'It's a variety of schizo-phrenia... It's a technical expression for something very simple – the good and evil in every man's soul.' Their remedy – attend church.

After attempting to rescue a young woman from a wolf attack, Larry Talbot (Chaney) begins his transformation as a pair of hairy legs become increasingly hairier – thanks to a series of lap dissolves. Head of Makeup Jack Pierce went for facial mobility over realism when creating his look, although Chaney is virtually unrecognisable under the snout and many layers of yak hair that took around six hours to apply.

This wasn't Pierce's first attempt at visualising a werewolf, though. He was responsible for Universal's less financially successful, but arguably eerier, monster, *Werewolf in London* (dir. Stuart Walker, 1935).

Echoing the *Little Red Riding Hood* legend, Talbot's werewolf strikes in fantastical woods, the full moon acting as his guiding light and, in this case, plenty of dry ice swirling around as atmospheric mist. As the characters regularly quote: 'Even a man who is pure in heart and says his prayers by night may become a wolf when the wolf's-bane blooms and the autumn moon is bright.'

Shivers (1975)

Director: David Cronenberg, Canada

Even before the AIDS virus had whipped the First World into a state of paranoid frenzy, filmmaker David Cronenberg was doing his best to pre-empt such happenings with this early career work, *Shivers*.

Set in a well-to-do, high-rise apartment complex, the film charts the destruction caused by a rogue parasite that was originally developed to replace diseased organs, but now does a fine job of turning its human hosts into sexually voracious sociopaths. As such, the self-contained apartment structure becomes the perfect incubator for this aggressive parasite, wreaking havoc in what is a cunning twist on the term 'free love'.

Commenting on human evolution, mutability of the body and the relationship between humankind and technology, *Shivers* is a queasy precursor to such apocalyptic treatises as *28 Days Later*, as well as Cronenberg's next feature, *Rabid* (1977).

In *Rabid*, Cronenberg utilises the acting talents of porn queen Marilyn Chambers, who, as the victim of a motorcycle crash, emerges from hospital with a hunger for sex and an unfortunate growth in her armpit. Orgiastic depravity ensues.

While both films straddle the line between this book's chapters on 'Monsters Spreading the Monster Disease' and 'Man-Made Monsters', one thing is gospel: they will grow on you.

EMMA WESTWOOD

Dog Soldiers (2002)

Director: Neil Marshall, UK/Luxembourg

Despite opening with a muddling ensemble sequence where each army-attired character looks just like the other one, *Dog Soldiers* quickly evolves into a biting werewolf horror/thriller with decidedly more grunt than comparatively less energetic projects like *An American Werewolf in London* (1981). The film was given the marketing tagline of '*Jaws*, *Aliens* and *Predator* with a werewolf twist'.

Filmmaker Neil Marshall's debut sees a team of British soldiers accosted by wild creatures while performing manoeuvres in the Scottish Highlands. Desperate, they seek refuge in a local farmhouse; however, their safety is very quickly compromised, with the werewolves staging repeated attacks against the property.

Starring son-of-Doctor-Who Sean Pertwee, *Dog Soldiers* sunk into an early grave in the US with a direct-to-video release – unfortunate for a film that sports some seriously scary werewolf effects that come to life on the big screen. Similarly, Marshall's second feature, the dark and incredibly claustrophobic *The Descent* – with its torch-lit cave dwellers – looks too muddy on DVD.

Dog Soldiers is full of nerdy film references too, including a nod to *The Evil Dead* filmmaker Sam Raimi – with one of the characters called Bruce Campbell.

From the Desk of...
Greg McLean
(Australia)

'With his icy stare, scratchy beard and cackling laugh, this is a monster without an ounce of human compassion.' — review of *Wolf Creek* by James Greenberg, *The Hollywood Reporter* (28 January 2005)

Filmography: *Wolf Creek* (2005), *Rogue* (2007)

Rogue is kind of the George-and-the-Dragon myth, a retelling of that story — not literally, more inspired by the Christian view of culture, the view of slaying the dragon to defend the society. It's about the notion of the dragon in Western civilisation, taken from Arthurian legends, where it's the representation of restraining forces in the human psychology. So the dragon in classical tales of the West is seen as keeping the damsel in distress captive in a castle and the knight then has to slay the dragon to save the princess or take the curse off the kingdom.

It's the opposite in Eastern culture because, in Eastern culture, the dragon is seen as a liberating force. It's not a scary force at all. So I'm interested in exploring the Western ideal, which is the tyrannical kind of force. And also a crocodile — a rogue crocodile, which has a personality of a big, old, male, horrible, bitter character, who sits in his dark, little place and keeps reign over a particular plot of dirt – that is like a dragon.

The story of *Rogue* is about a modern guy (Michael Vartan) who lives in a modern environment, who is out of touch with his own inner self. Through encountering the dragon at the end of the story, he releases a part of himself that he thought he had lost. *Rogue* has that kind of mythic resonance. Of course, it's up to the audience whether that's clear to them, but hopefully it registers on a subconscious level. If they keep thinking about it longer than the experience of seeing the film, then it's had an impact.

Creating a human monster like Mick Taylor (John Jarratt in *Wolf Creek*) was completely different to creating the animal in *Rogue*. When it's an animal, it's about identifying what that creature might represent. The fear. A shark is all about the body down beneath the surface, what's happening under the water that you can't see. That's the huge terror. The crocodile is very different because it's about something that is very smart, that is stalking you, that is playing a game with you. It's very different to the shark fear. It's something that could potentially out-smart you.

With human monsters, like Mick Taylor, the fear is about seeing someone who looks a certain way, then changes, and you find a monster face under the mask. That's the Hannibal Lecter kind of idea, essentially dealing with a human being – a sociopath, a psychopath – someone who appears completely normal, but is not. Like all those serial killers you hear about… You know, the ones where the neighbours say, 'He was such a nice guy,' yet he's dismembering people and drinking their blood. The human monster is the person who has always been a monster, but wears the mask of a human being. Mick Taylor is that. He captures that.

I think there are human monsters that definitely fall under the category of a monster, a monster personality. You could say that Hitler was a monster – someone who appears to have the mask of civility, but is unleashing such horrific, evil tyranny and with a complete lack of compassion for humanity.

When you have a human being who can operate without any understanding of another human being's pain and suffering, you've got a monster. That was a big thing when creating Mick Taylor – realising that he's really based on the serial killer Ivan Milat. He's an individual who can separate himself from that empathy and, if you can remove your empathy and compassion, you can be a monster. This is where big business can also be a monster because, sometimes, they're destroying communities and so forth and they just don't get the concept – or care – that this is real life.

I wrote *Rogue* a long time ago. When I was trying to get it going the first time – because I had a couple of attempts at getting it made – I took a trip up to the Northern Territory for two weeks and rented a car and got some camping stuff and went around all the crocodile hotspots. I went on the actual boat trip they take in the film and that was incredible.

All the stuff I put in the movie was pretty close to being accurate – what crocodiles do, how they behave, the land-scape up there, that kind of stuff. Later, when the film got up and running, I went to the crocodile farms and got in-depth behavioural info. When we went back to shoot the film, we sent the visual effects crew and one of the other producers up there for a while. They spent a month with the crocodile handlers, talking about whether they would do this, could they do this... just to make our creature seem like a real animal rather than just a silly monster. The idea was to make him as believable as possible.

From the very start, I knew that *Rogue* was about having real, sentient characters interacting with a real crocodile. I told my crew that the crocodile has to be realistic and it can't be doing anything that makes you not believe it. Basically, if it feels phoney, let's not include it.

Another thing I told everyone was, in terms of all the crocodiles I've seen in movies, I've never seen one that looks real. If you look at crocodiles in the wild, they are incredibly simple animals that don't really do much. When you see them in movies, they are always jumping around like puppy dogs. In reality, they just sit there until it's time to kill, then they move. They just sit on the banks with their mouths open.

I said that we have to remove all of that phoney movement – audiences just know because they've seen The Discovery Channel, they've seen Animal Planet. Filmmakers have tried to characterise the crocodile personality by making them evil – by giving them a little raised, evil-eye thing. But what they don't realise is that just looks stupid. No animal looks like that. If you present them as they are – with the stillness and the staring – that's scarier than trying to put human characteristics on an animal that's already scary.

With a monster movie that's an animal film – I imagine like the *Alien* movie – 90 per cent of how scared the audience is of the creature is how scared the actors acting against it are. You can have fantastic visual effects, but if you've got bad acting, it doesn't matter – it will actually decrease the quality of the visual effects because the audience is looking at the real emotion in the actors.

I was really careful to cast really good actors and ensure they completely believed in the crocodile. They sell it to such a degree that, if you look at the acting in a film like *Jaws*, the shark often looks crap – or not even there – but their performances create it in your mind. That's what actually makes a great monster movie.

Spielberg was a genius with that kind of cinematic language. His greatest shots are the reaction shots, even though he does great visual effects as well. That sells the effect. What was also clever about *Jaws* was they made it about 'this' shark. It's not just a shark movie – it's about this one. That shark had a bad nature, which is really interesting because it is a fish and, I mean, how much personality can a fish really have? But there's this great line when Quinn looks down and says, 'It's a bad fish,' and you can sense that this one is particularly evil. It's educational for today's monster moviemakers how little we see the monster, but how powerful it still is.

In terms of movie monsters, my favourites are *Jaws*, *Alien*, *Creature from the Black Lagoon*, the original *Frankenstein*... all the old Universal horror films, things like *Dracula* and *The Wolf Man*. I grew up loving those movies. There's something very iconic about each one of those monsters and, thematically, they're about different things.

There's a great book by Stephen King called *Danse Macabre* that's, basically, about this guy who spends his whole life thinking about trying to scare people, and fear, and what it is. It's his kind of riff on what he thinks horror is all about. Everyone who's making horror films should really read it. It says there are three or four different kinds of monsters that all monsters fall under, no matter what movie it is or what character it is. Essentially, these films draw from the werewolf myth, the Dracula myth, the Frankenstein myth in some form or the other, definitely in what they represent psychologically.

The crocodile comes from the same category as the shark – it's basically an external force of nature. The fear is that there's something in nature that's going to rip your whole world apart. The 70s saw a great bunch of these films about nature turning against us. It's a perennial thing in horror, which is ultimately a bit of a Frankenstein myth as well because, it's saying, if you try to play God, you'll create a monster... and the monster will turn against you.

Is there room in this day and age to create a truly unique monster? Well, you've got to go back to the core ideas of the form. *The Host* is a great example. In one sense, it's a monster movie, but it's actually a very emotional story of a family, so it's flipping that whole concept on its head. Any film form can be given a shot in the arm at any time. It's a matter of filmmakers looking at it for what it really is. The bad ones don't add anything to the form and just slavishly conform to the trends. When someone comes along and, basically, strips it all back and says what it really is about on a psychological level, they're putting truth and originality into it.

Rogue isn't about a crocodile. It's about a group of people and their reaction to things. Making monster movies, you don't want to make it about the monster. The monster is a metaphor for something else. Usually, the good monster movies are about something else. *The Exorcist* isn't about the devil. It's about the family and how they survive that situation. Good movies are always about something we can relate to. They tell a story that – hopefully – taps into a deeper human truth and allows an audience to participate in that, sometimes, terrifying idea from the safety of their cinema seat.

They Come in Peace... Or Do They?
Monsters from Outer Space

The Universe is a mighty big place, big enough to support life on Earth and, presumably, a trillion or so other varieties of intelligent (or otherwise) beings. Once upon a time, fears were that 'they' would come to conquer us, but with the initiation of the space race, we're now travelling to them. And it's more likely than not that our welcome won't be one with open arms.

Alien (1979)

Director: Ridley Scott, USA

A cultural theorist's wet dream, *Alien* is one of the most talked-about, frame-by-frame dissected and academically flogged films in modern cinema. Which means one thing: we're only going to touch on the film's rich history in a 700-word appraisal.

Considering everyone has so much to say about *Alien*, the film itself is pure simplicity – sparse dialogue, a strong setting, a tension-building linear storyline... Really, you don't get simpler than this, and you don't get closer to perfection. Those students in film schools everywhere who've had the

'KISS' (i.e. 'keep it simple, stupid') methodology rammed down their throats need only do one thing: watch *Alien* and learn.

As the vehicle that launched Sigourney Weaver's career and sent her on a journey that would survive many sequels as the character Ellen Ripley, *Alien* has been widely acknowledged for groundbreaking feminism (it's one of the first Hollywood action movies featuring a lead heroine), while others have argued that it's actually misogynistic. But enough of the academia or we'll be here for the rest of the book.

Belying its production values and box-office blitz, *Alien* was made on the cheap by filmmaking standards (approx. US$11 million), proving that imagination goes further than the dollar. Even the so-called 'development' of CG effects in today's market doesn't come close to the inventiveness of the Mother alien. Powerful stuff.

Physicality: As a designer, the Swiss surrealist H.R. Giger is so much more than merely his 'alien' design, as wonderful as it is.

Giger's official website describes his work as having a 'biomechanical aesthetic', which is clarified as 'a dialectic between man and machine, representing a universe at once disturbing and sublime'. True. He's also a painter, sculptor, interior architect and – these days – even a jeweller, but he'll be remembered by the wider consciousness for his outstanding visualisation of *Alien*'s titular character, for which he also won an Oscar.

The Mother alien – the monster – is an all-encompassing being that, following her gestation within the snuggly confines of a crew member's chest (bursting forth in *that* bloody scene, which purportedly took the cast unawares), becomes as ubiquitous as the space craft itself. Her machine-cum-human, statuesque form – an oily black in colour – can entwine itself in the ship's intestines, which makes her attacks unexpected at the best of times. She has acid as blood, deathly claws and a phallic set of protruding chompers.

Yes, she is a superb creature, made even more fascinating by her speed and patience. In fact, we never *really* see her properly until the film's sequel, which indicates remarkable restraint by director Ridley Scott because she is really something to behold.

Personality: A parasitical creature, the Mother alien lays a large nest of eggs that hatch whenever an unsuspecting soft body leans over for a closer look. A 'face-hugger' contained within the egg then suffocates its host, acting as the host's oxygen source while they exist in a sustainable coma. The little baby alien is aggressively birthed through the host's chest, surviving on the flesh of other beings, and so the cycle goes.

Like any mother, the alien will sacrifice herself in order to protect her young. In this way, she is like anyone else, but otherwise, her primary instincts are to attack, propagate the species and conquer. She doesn't speak, only screeches.

Lineage and Legacy: *Alien*'s auteur, Ridley Scott, quit the film franchise while he was ahead, but kudos to James Cameron for his stunning sequel *Aliens* (1986), which functions more as an action film while the original was horror. As Scott had pioneered, Cameron continued the strong ensemble vibe, the result being a noteworthy standalone feature despite the inherent pressure in following up Scott's work of perfection.

Unfortunately, the genius ended with Cameron's film, although director David Fincher (*Se7en*) is better than his work in *Alien 3* (1992), and the same goes for Jean-Pierre Jeunet (*Amélie*) and writer Joss Whedon (*Buffy the Vampire Slayer*) with *Alien: Resurrection* (1997). The alien creature eventually crossed over to battle other monsters in *Alien vs. Predator* (2004) and *Alien vs. Predator: Requiem* (2007).

Alien's influence hasn't ended with a few sequels, though. While some films are better than others, John Carpenter's *The Thing* (see below) is a beautiful homage to *Alien*, as opposed to being a rip-off. But *Alien* itself isn't as original as it may originally seem; in fact, the influencer was influenced by a number of sources. Screenwriter Dan O'Bannon has openly admitted being inspired by *The Thing from Another World* (1951), *Forbidden Planet* (p.145) and *It! The Terror from Beyond Space* (1958, p.153), among other early sci-fi.

The Thing (1982)

Director: John Carpenter, USA

Made within three years of each other, there are more than a few similarities between *Alien* and *The Thing* – a parasitical creature from outer space never before discovered, a team of people under extreme emotional pressure, a suffocating sense of isolation and being trapped far from home... blah, blah, blah.

While 'imitation' could be the word that springs to mind, in this case it's actually proof that a *really* strong concept has far more potential than that of just one movie. In the hands of someone with creative smarts, it can be massaged into a different form, into an original piece using ostensibly the same prototype. Enter John Carpenter...

The first film in Carpenter's self-proclaimed 'Apocalypse Trilogy' – incorporating *Prince of Darkness* (1987) and *In the Mouth of Madness* (1995) – *The Thing* was unjustly usurped at the box office by the release of the feel-good, family alien flick, *E.T.: The Extra Terrestrial* and, ironically, *Alien* director Ridley Scott's other masterwork, *Blade Runner*, which was released on the same day. But *The Thing* was always going to be an acquired taste anyway.

Despite having an extremely accessible and exciting story-line – that of an American Antarctica research station being infiltrated by a shape-changing alien life-force dug out of the ice – special-effects genius Rob Bottin did too much of a good job. His alien was so gruesome, with such uncompromised gore, he managed to scare people away. Bottin's visuals also earned him a review from Roger Ebert that called his effects 'among the most elaborate, nauseating, and horrifying sights yet achieved by Hollywood's new generation of visual magicians'.

The Thing is a cinematic rollercoaster ride and one that you won't purchase a ticket for lightly, but once you do, you'll want to hop on again and again. This author is clocking up well over 20 viewings... and it's still thrilling.

Physicality: The big question here is: what does this 'thing' look like? See, that's the problem. Many thousands of years in age, it's a thing of undetermined size and appearance. It's a slimy sludge-fest of flesh and organs both on the inside and out, but when dormant it hides in either human or animal form, camouflaged as its host until it's time to move to the next body. That's when we see it – when its hiding place is compromised or when it's time to move to the next thing.

When the 'thing' appears, it's bursting from a body in some disconcertingly antagonistic manner – a head detaching itself from a torso then oozing off a table of its own accord, growing legs that send it scuttling across the floor; the turning of a man's chest into a bear-trap-like cavity that then devours the arms of a doctor attempting to perform emergency CPR. You get the picture.

To say that Rob Bottin outdid himself with the special effects in *The Thing* is an understatement. The 22-year-old was so dedicated to the project that he worked himself into a state of exhaustion. In fact, Stan Winston completed some of the creature work in the dog cage scene while Bottin was in recovery.

Personality: *The Thing's* creature has one thing on its 'mind': complete annihilation of all other species. Given time, it will systematically work itself around the world. As far as personality goes, it has none, except that of its host. Everyone on the remote research station becomes a suspect because the extent of this monster's shape shifting ability means that it is undetectable... well, almost.

Lineage and Legacy: John Carpenter's idea of *The Thing* came from a pulp-back novella, *Who Goes There?*, published in 1938 by John W. Campbell. Before Carpenter picked up on the whole (pardon the pun) thing, though, producer Howard Hawks and director Christian Nyby took a stab at it with the sci-fi cult classic, *The Thing from Another World* (1951) – see influences on *Alien* (p.139).

Even though Carpenter was a fan of the 1951 version of *The Thing*, he drew more from the plot of the novella for his screen adaptation. And even though this book has chosen to spotlight the Carpenter film, take heed, Hawks's film should be added to any list of serious investigation into monster movies.

The finale of Carpenter's *The Thing* leaves it open to sequels, but for the last 25 years, the film has existed as a single feature. There's been talk of a prequel and even a remake around Hollywood circles; however, time will tell. No hurry. *The Thing* is complete as it stands and there's no need to try and improve on it.

Forbidden Planet (1956)

Director: Fred McLeod Wilcox, USA

The classic of classic 50s sci-fi, *Forbidden Planet* not only marks the big-screen debut of Robby the Robot – who would go on to enjoy a stellar career of his own, most famously seen in TV's *Lost in Space* series – but presents an omnipotent monster of a unique persuasion: an invisible one.

Considering the intergalactic setting, which informs the film from start to finish, it seems appropriate to discuss *Forbidden Planet* under the 'Monsters from Outer Space' category, although this oblique creature is more human than viewers will initially anticipate and, therefore, comfortable under a couple of other categories in this book. Mum's the word on that, so as not to spoil the experience for the uninitiated.

What's so wonderful about this film – apart from Louis and Bebe Barron's soundtrack of zips, pings and zings (otherwise known as 'electronic tonalities') – is the glorious painted sets and backdrops that echo the halcyon days of Alfred Hitchcock's mid-career, i.e. so obviously fake, but so breathtakingly beautiful at the same time.

A crew of space travellers in the final decade of the twenty-first century, headed by Leslie Nielsen as their captain, investigate the outcome of an expedition to a planet located 16 light-years from Earth. When they approach, one of the expedition's sole survivors, Dr Morbius (Walter Pidgeon), warns them not to land, yet they ignore his request. What they find is a pastel-hued utopia, full of roaming animals, but where the majority of inhabitants have mysteriously died in violent circumstances.

While Dr Morbius prides himself on his civility and an IQ that would place him beyond mere genius, he's actually more primitive than first impressions.

Physicality: Considering this monster is invisible, there's not a lot to say in terms of his physicality. He first reveals himself to an officer through his breathing, and then footprints in the soil allow the crew to calculate his size and supposed appearance.

Doc says he 'runs counter to every law of adaptive evolution' and that his clawed foot of approximately 37 by 19 inches looks like it belongs to some sort of tree sloth. Whatever he may look like, though – and we get an animated relief of his outline when he gets caught in the electric perimeter that acts as security for their spacecraft – he's impervious to atomic fissure guns, which leads them to believe he can renew his molecular structure from one second to the next.

While the invisibility hides his bulky size and allows for a stealthy attack, his ability to melt steel like butter would suggest that, even if detectable to the eye, this monster would be no pushover anyway.

Personality: Just like Mr Hyde (see *Dr Jekyll & Mr Hyde*, p.45), this monster doesn't take too kindly to new acquaintances. As soon as the space crew starts to threaten the peaceful equilibrium on the planet, Dr Morbius laments: 'It's happening again.'

There's just no stopping this angry monster once he gets something in his head. His objective: to tear all intruders limb from limb.

Lineage and Legacy: Colourful and clever, *Forbidden Planet* has been credited with influencing a whole bundle of science fiction television shows and movies over the decades. In fact, it has even been referred to as 'the first episode of *Star Trek*', with *Star Trek* creator Gene Roddenberry noting the film's inspiration in his biography.

Everything from *The Blob* (see below) to *Halloween* has referenced *Forbidden Planet*, and, considering its status of intellectual camp, it looks set to be referenced further in more movies as the twenty-first century unfolds.

The Blob (1958)

Director: Irvin S. Yeaworth Jr, USA

When it comes to jaunty theme songs, *The Blob* is a winner by a country mile. The film's catchy tune with lyrics that go something like *'Beware of the Blob... It creeps and leaps and glides and slides across the floor...'* establishes a bubble-gum pop feel to the film, contrary to it being a genuine sci-fi horror flick – and one that would have teenagers jumping into the arms of their sweethearts at drive-ins state-wide.

The Blob's title song also achieved notoriety by being an early work from Burt Bacharach who, for the uninitiated, is one of the most accomplished song composers of the twentieth century. As for the film's incidental score, that comes courtesy of Ralph Carmichael, who was known as 'The Dean of Contemporary Christian Music'.

But there's more to *The Blob* than a tune you'll be whistling for weeks afterwards. Marketed towards a teenage audience, the film hones in on a misunderstood generation of youth who, by drag racing and attending midnight spook flicks, are labelled juvenile delinquents by a community's pig-headed 'adults'.

When a young couple (including Steve McQueen in his debut film role) raises the alarm that something has gone horribly wrong at a doctor's office, they find themselves the subject of suspicion – after all, nobody is going to believe that an amorphous creature from outer space is attacking the local community. Soon the Blob is too big to ignore, though, and the hysteria begins.

There is many a cute moment in *The Blob*, particularly the scene of the Blob's most significant mass attack – a cinema ('healthfully' air-conditioned), which, of course, is exactly the place where the audience of the time would be watching the film. This cinema is featuring the fictional movie *The Vampire and the Robot*.

Physicality: After plummeting to Earth in a meteorite, the Blob starts as a seemingly harmless baby blob that resembles the 'slime' kids' product that was popular in the 1970s/80s. But let it drip down onto your hand and it takes on a life of its own, drawing sustenance from whatever flesh it consumes and, consequently, growing larger.

As the Blob absorbs people, it turns a deep red in colour and looks like a rolling ball of resin that can flatten itself to ooze under doors, through air vents and cinema bio-box windows. Towards the finale of the film, it is big enough to completely engulf a house. It is also impervious to bullets and whatever acid you can throw at it, so, as far as everyone is concerned, it's invincible.

Personality: There's not much going on here in terms of personality. The Blob doesn't even have a mouth to talk, grunt or groan – or eyes to throw you an evil stare – which means the only way it connects with its victims is by sliming them. Intellectually unstimulating.

Lineage and Legacy: *The Blob* ends with a strong suggestion that this story is not over. A sequel did eventuate, but not until some time later – *Beware! The Blob* (1972). Then the original film was remade in 1988.

Even though director Irvin Yeaworth was purportedly never proud of his creation, it has survived as one of the quintessential 1950s American horror/sci-fi films, which some may say is a much greater achievement than the 400 shorts he produced for religious and motivational purposes. Although, let's not forget, Yeaworth did make another foray into monsterdom with *Dinosaurus!* in 1960.

As if to cement its importance to the teen culture of its time, scenes from *The Blob* appeared in the musical *Grease* (1978).

Pitch Black (2000)

Director: David Twohy, Australia/USA

Pitch Black does its best to buy into the ingrained fear of the dark that we humans have nurtured since our childhoods. Ironically, though, the film starts in over-exposed sunshine when a cargo spacecraft caught in a meteor shower makes an emergency landing on a desert planet.

With three suns, this planet rarely experiences nightfall – only once every 22 years, to be exact – so the characters walk around in a bleached-out, burnt-up world with very little colour. Unluckily for them, they've arrived in time for that 22-year lunar eclipse, which means they're also going to get acquainted with the planet's other inhabitants: predatory flying aliens who, despite being remarkably hardy and hostile, cower from the light and only surface when it's dark.

The most well-known project from director David Twohy – who largely works as a screenwriter (*Waterworld* and *G.I Jane* form part of his résumé) – *Pitch Black* features a smattering of Australian actors, most of whom hide their pedigree by speaking in thick American accents.

While the film opens on an adrenaline-charged crash sequence, it really comes into its own as soon as the night falls and these *Alien*-inspired creatures start flying out of their burrows in their thousands like a swarm of locusts. Despite their arrival being something of an apocalyptic sign, the

character of Riddick (Vin Diesel) is even forced to acknowl-
edge their awakening as 'beautiful'.

Physicality: Initially, Riddick – a hard-as-nails prisoner
convicted for murder – functions as the monster of the film.
Riddick is big, brooding and cold as ice, which means the
rest of the ship's passengers are extremely wary of him,
considering him to be the greatest threat to their safety.

As if to add insult to injury, he has spooky night-vision
eyes – the result of a prison 'shine job' to help him see in his
dark cell – which sets him apart even further as someone
'different'. His physical aberration proves to be a gift, though,
when it comes to fighting the nocturnal aliens. You could call
him, the 'Rudolph the Red-Nosed Reindeer' of the bunch.

The aliens are referred to as 'bioraptors' or 'bad boys' (in
the words of Riddick). Bat-like in their ability to fly, but
larger, they communicate with each other like dolphins in
strange echoing tones, which one character believes is their
way of seeing. If you don't move a muscle, then these fellows
have a tough time locating you.

Speed is another characteristic of the bioraptors – a
running person has no hope of escaping a pretty vicious
slicing-and-dicing. Their speed makes it hard for us, as an
audience, to lock onto detail of their physical shape, although
bits and pieces emerge, such as blade-sharp limbs that look
like manufactured tools.

Personality: Without intruders to hunt and kill, one
wonders what these creatures would actually be doing come
the 22-year eclipse. Considering the ferocity of their
onslaught, a game of poker seems out of the question.

At one stage, Riddick says, 'Check your cuts – these bad boys know our blood now.' So it appears that hunting vulnerable humans is a kind of sport for them, and there is no sense appealing to their mercy.

The bioraptors don't even show remorse for each other. When the characters, swathed in tubes of neon light, attempt to cross an open space, they feel droplets of blue blood raining down on top of them, which is the creatures attacking each other from above. Blue blood? Could there be a message here?

Lineage and Legacy: *Pitch Black* managed to secure a nice little following for both the film and the character of Riddick, who Vin Diesel embodies perfectly.

To this day, the legacy of the film continues with home-console games, a short animated film, a prequel that was supposed to be a documentary and a sequel called *The Chronicles of Riddick* (2004), also directed by David Twohy.

And Then Some...

20 Million Miles to Earth (1957)

Director: Nathan Juran, USA

Known predominantly to fans through *Jason and the Argonauts* (p.31) and *The Seventh Voyage of Sinbad* (p.23), *20 Million Miles to Earth* is special-effects iconoclast Ray Harryhausen's more earnest film – his 'thinking man's monster movie' – and his homage to the film that inspired his career: *King Kong*.

Just like Kong and Frankenstein, Harryhausen's Ymir is the

proverbial 'fish out of water' that finds itself displaced in a foreign world. This Ymir, although only referred to as 'the creature' in the film, is marooned on Earth after being salvaged by the first manned spacecraft to Venus, which crash-lands near a Sicilian fishing village when making its return.

Hatching from an egg, the Ymir starts life very small and benevolent, with no interest in harming its human captors – in fact, it appears to be an herbivore. This sympathetic being only turns aggressive when others torment it; external factors impacting on an otherwise docile personality.

While Kong scaled the Empire State Building, 'the creature' rampages through Rome's historic Colosseum in the tragic finale of the film. As Harryhausen says, 'Man destroys what he doesn't understand.' So true, even to this day.

It! The Terror from Beyond Space (1958)

Director: Edward L. Cahn, USA

Set in 'the future' (i.e. 2009), *It! The Terror from Beyond Space* was one of the primary inspirations for the sci-fi hit *Alien* – to the extent that *Alien*'s 'homage' invoked the ire of the producers of *It!* See if you can spot the similarities.

A vessel is sent to perform the space rescue of a mission exploring Mars. When they arrive, only one survivor greets them, and they consequently suspect him of having murdered the others. He pleads his ignorance, insisting that an unknown creature is responsible for the deaths.

The commander of the rescue mission is distrustful, so they take off for Earth, unaware that this Martian has now snuck aboard their ship. Their journey home becomes a game of survival as the body count mounts and the creature – who draws his nourishment from their fluids – proves impervious to an arsenal of weaponry. Without giving too much away, let's just say the conclusion is very similar to *Alien*.

Designed by Paul Blaisdal, whose monster creations included *Attack of the Puppet People* (1958) and *The She Creature* (1956), the Martian of *It!* was originally intended to be left to the imagination, but instead appears as a green, reptilian guy in a rubber suit. Good stuff, regardless.

Starship Troopers (1997)

Director: Paul Verhoeven, USA

Apart from being an infinitely entertaining, retro-futuristic actioner, *Starship Troopers* is a seething social satire, highly original and bleak despite its sunny overtones and chiselled cast (including a very scary Denise Richards).

As far as the story goes – based on a novel by Robert A. Heinlein, a well-known right-wing apologist – a group of starry-eyed graduates, pumped up with patriotism and the quest to become 'citizens', engage in active service against an invading race of intelligent alien bugs called 'Arachnids'.

Considering the light disposition of this film, the first hand-to-hand conflict between humans and bugs really makes you sit back and take notice. As conceived by Phil Tippett, these spindly creatures skewer and slice through human flesh like it's papier-mâché, while other larger and more stag-beetle-looking varieties shoot spaceship-destroying meteorites into the air.

Later, we meet some flying, wasp-like mutations that have the razor talons to lop off heads, and the granddaddy of the bugs – a bloated witchetty-grub-like, brain-sucking slug that, as is the case with many horrifying monsters, bears some likeness to female genitalia. Totally rad.

Not of this Earth (1957)

Director: Roger Corman, USA

Considered one of Roger Corman's winning works – amid an oeuvre that oscillates between genius and trash – *Not of this Earth* centres on an aloof fellow who engages the services of a nurse while undergoing constant blood transfusions. Of course, his highly unusual condition piques the curiosity of a doctor, who discovers that this man is, actually, not a man at all, but a vampiric alien sent to start the ball rolling on a worldwide takeover by leaching the blood from Earthlings in order to help save his dying race.

This seemingly mild-mannered gentleman hides his pupil-less, death-ray eyes behind wraparound sunglasses, and manages to retain a sense of menace despite his physical fragility.

With a 67-minute running time, *Not of this Earth* proves you don't need a *Lord of the Rings*-style epic to make an impression. The film has been remade twice – in 1988, starring former porn star Traci Lords, and in 1995 with Michael York.

Predator (1987)

Director: John McTiernan, USA

Action filmmaker John McTiernan (*Die Hard*) pits a beefy Arnold Schwarzenegger against an extra-terrestrial warrior in this full-throttle, sci-fi thriller.

Turning the tables so that the hunter becomes the hunted, a team of commandos in the Central American jungle think they're on a mission to rescue airmen captured by guerrillas, but soon find themselves pawns in a blood-and-guts battle. Their 'opponent' is a largely invisible alien humanoid, who has come to Earth to indulge in a spot of exotic game hunting, which, in this case, means tracking down humans.

Not much is known about 'the predator' in this film, although a sequel called *Predator 2* (1990) and the hybrid sequels *Alien vs. Predator* (2004) and *Alien vs. Predator: Requiem* (2007) filled in many of the gaps in the back-story. It was reported that Jean-Claude Van Damme was meant to wear the predator suit, but was considered not sufficiently physically imposing to trump the likes of Schwarzenegger and Carl Weathers. Instead, the seven-foot-two Kevin Peter Hall (Sasquatch in *Harry and the Hendersons*) was hired as Arnie's opponent.

Adrenaline-pumping fun.

From the Desk of...
John Carpenter
(USA)

'There are times when we seem to be sticking our heads right down into the bloody, stinking maw of the unknown, as the Thing transforms itself into creatures with the body parts of dogs, men, lobsters, and spiders, all wrapped up in gooey intestine.' – review of *The Thing* by Roger Ebert, *Chicago Sun Times* (1 January 1982)

Filmography: *Dark Star* (1974), *The Thing* (1982), *Christine* (1983), *Prince of Darkness* (1987), *They Live* (1988), *In the Mouth of Madness* (1995), *Village of the Damned* (1995), *Vampires* (1998)

Growing up in the 50s, that's the time I remember and love the most as a moviegoer. I think you always love the movies you see when you're young. Always. They make this gigantic impression on you.

In the United States, they just released a DVD of old monster films made during the 1950s. Watching this DVD is like taking my favourite drugs. I love it. There are four movies in there and they're just awful... *The Gigantic Claw* (1957), *The Werewolf* (1956), *Zombies of Mora Tau* (1957) and

The Creature With The Atom Brain (1955). They're terrible but fabulous. God, yeah.

The 50s was a great time for monster movies and science-fiction movies. That was the time of the giant-bug movies – *Them!, Tarantula, Beginning of the End*. My love of monster movies goes very, very deep. During the 50s, they were re-releasing the classics – Universal classics like *Dracula, Frankenstein, The Wolf Man* – on television. It was just wonderful. When the occasional film came along that purported to be a monster movie, but was really not, it pissed me off.

Monsters are glorious because, first up, you want to know what they look like. That was the big thing when I was a kid. If they made a great-looking monster, it was so fabulous. 'Show me my monster, guys. I want to see it. I don't want it to be in the dark. I want it to come out in the light. I want to see this bastard. I want to deal with it on the screen. I don't want it to be a dog in makeup like *The Hound of the Baskervilles*. Give me my monster and give it to me now!' That was my attitude. Just as long as you give me a glimpse of the monster, then I'm a happy camper.

Monster movies have been with us since the beginning of cinema. They're nothing new. Monster films keep getting, essentially, reinvented with every generation. Each time there's a change in calendar, we're all getting older, and a monster movie will come out and we think we're seeing something new.

Monster tales are ancient. Go back to the time when we climbed out of the trees, formed tribes and were hunter-gatherers. We'd sit around campfires and talk about evil, and get worried about those terrible monsters out there in the dark – monsters that may come and get us.

Monsters are manifestations of us. They can be us in different terms. They can represent things as they do in fables and myths and fairytales. They keep evolving throughout time. They've always been important in terms of any type of cultural myth that's going on – the monster is us in a different way, they're part of us. They could be our conscience, the dark part of humanity. You can see this from the very beginning, the earliest writings.

Monsters also come from people's knowledge of the world that they live in, and their ability to explain that world to others. Monsters are a way of putting it in symbolic and visceral terms so we can all understand.

Look at the myth of Dracula. Vampires have been around in one form or another for a long, long time. Dracula was a gothic romance about the end of the aristocracy in Europe. Vampires crumbled and they were bloodsuckers. They fed on people. They were corrupt. They hid in the dark. You see all these things and you say, 'I know what this is about.' The myth is basically talking about the end of aristocratic culture.

Now we keep reinventing vampires, over and over and over again. Béla Lugosi – he was Dracula and generally followed the idea of Dracula from the Stoker book. He was the embodiment of a 1930s, swooning, silent-movies sexuality. It was the 30s, he had this thick accent... It looks cheesy to us now, right? But at the time, it was like, 'Oh my, what a sensation.' But now look at vampires... Vampires don't really change, they just change their costumes. We add a few details, like day-walkers and all that crap, but they do exactly the same things – that never changes. They're a durable myth. They're wonderful.

Monstrous behaviour in humans is what monsters represent in movies. Monsters themselves are, essentially, mythical
creatures that are non-human creatures. Human beings that
display monstrous behaviour, as in *Wolf Creek*, they're even
more terrifying sometimes. They hit closer to home in terms
of the horror. I mean, it's harder to understand the darkness
in each of us.

A monster movie has a monster in it – a mystical creature,
whether that comes from outer space, or whether it's created
by a doctor with lightning, or it's an ancient legend like the
vampire or a wendigo (a malevolent cannibalistic spirit into
which humans can be transformed), or all sorts of things. But
they're supernatural in one way or another. They're above
nature. They're not a part of everyday nature. A man walking
down the street might be monstrous, but he's not a monster
– he's human.

There have been quite a few monsters in my movies. *Prince
of Darkness*... *In the Mouth of Madness* has a bunch of
monsters in it. *They Live*... well, they're aliens, but I guess
you can call them monsters. My first film, *Dark Star*, had a
cheese-ball monster in it.

The Thing was offered to me as an assignment by Universal
and it was my first studio film. I was a big fan of the original
movie – *The Thing from Another World* – it terrified me. Oh
God, it was scary. I had mixed feelings at first because of my
love for the original film, but it was vastly different to the
novella upon which it was based – *Who Goes There?* by John
W. Campbell – about a creature who imitates humans
perfectly so you can't tell who is imitation and who is real.

The Thing is a purely evil monster, but, on the other hand,
all it's trying to do is survive. So it's about survival instinct,

160

which we all hopefully have. It's evil in our world. It's evil to us because it hides in us.

How did I conceive a monster like the one in *The Thing*? I found someone able to design and build it – Rob Bottin. He came up with how to do it and the idea behind it, which is a great idea – it can look like anything. It comes along and imitates, then it shows you every life form it's ever imitated, on however many planets it's ever been on. So it's not one Thing we're looking at, it's not one creature that looks like 'this'. It's not like Frankenstein who never changes. It looks like a hundred million different things.

Essentially, the challenge was to design something that can be executed with special makeup and effects, which are right in front of camera. They're not computerised. They're rubbers operated by people. They're very effective because a computer does not animate them. The real-life movement is so disturbing. When the art of it, the sculpting, is realistic, it really looks like a human face. Really disturbing.

When it comes to CG effects, if you look at *Jurassic Park*, that's extremely successful. That film moved the art way beyond what was possible before. I mean, those dinosaurs running… all that stuff was incredible and, at the time, it was jaw-dropping. CG can be quite incredible, but it can also be quite ridiculous. It's just like anything else. I would pay a lot of money to see a special-makeup-effects person create a giant monster that moved around. It can't be done.

In the 80s in the United States, there was an enormous body culture starting up. People started to exercise. There was this worship of the body and an unease with the body too – that you might get fat and you might not be as attractive any more. Well, what we did with *The Thing* was throw it in people's faces

– take the human body and rip it apart as an attack on the body culture. That was there and also the virus and all that.

While Rob Bottin had a bunch of great ideas, he hadn't figured the whole thing out. He sort of figured it out as we went along, which is an extremely terrifying thing to do as a director. We didn't know what it was going to look like until the whole film was shot and we were shooting insert effects.

I don't know if I'd ever do that again as a director. I was young and stupid, I guess. When you don't know, you're just taking a big leap of faith, so it was like a religious experience – it was all about faith. I had faith that we would work it out, that we would find a way to go through it. And oftentimes, the designs would not work, so we'd have to go back and re-conceive them. This was going on as the movie was being shot. It was insane.

No one's really imitated *The Thing*, which is really interesting to me, because I don't know why. I agree that it's been really influential. It's so different. It's not like any other monster movie that I've ever seen. When shooting, I was just hoping we'd get something. We were walking in the dark.

Christine came about because *The Thing* was a pretty big failure in box-office terms. I was attacked for doing awful things because of the violence. The fans hated me, which serves me right for going down that path. They turned against me because they thought I had soiled the original. I should've realised, because they'll turn on you like bad pets – they'll bite you.

I needed a job and I'd missed out on a movie because of *The Thing*. And then along came *Christine*. It was a Stephen King book about a haunted car and I thought, 'What can we do with this?' If you love cars and you're a car-culture sort of person, then it's OK.

Village of the Damned came about because I had to finish off a contract with Universal. Once again, that was an assignment. I'd seen the original film in 1960. I think I had a thing for one of the little blonde girls – a 12-year-old thing, not an adult thing. I liked the original movie. There are a lot of great things about it, but there are a lot of stupid things about it too because it was of its time.

I went back to the original movie as much as possible – the brick-wall ending and the design of the kids is pretty much out of the original film. One of the issues, however, that I noticed about the original movie was that pregnancy was dealt with hilariously, like the wife (Barbara Shelly) had indigestion. It was so bizarre. The husband and wife live in this big mansion and she kind of goes off into another drawing room and comes back a bit later with a kid. It was hilarious so I thought we could update this a little. That was a fun movie to do – that was Christopher Reeve's last movie before his accident.

With my film *Vampires* – like I said before – they just have new clothes. Vampires never change, but the business around them changes. In terms of the monsters, I don't know what you can do to change that. That was good fun to make.

The one vampire film that stands out in my mind was a film I saw when I was ten. It was called *The Horror of Dracula* – a Hammer film. Christopher Lee played Dracula and it was just sensational. It sexualised the vampirism more than had been done before. The girls wanted 'it', if you know what I mean. She'd be in bed and she'd rip her bodice a bit in anticipation of his bite… It was great stuff. I'm telling you, for a young kid who was ten years old, that was hot and heavy, man. It's great. Plus the British, they love to have low-cut dresses. That was always a plus for us as kids.

I'm a big Godzilla fan. I believe I have all the movies. Every Godzilla film is brilliant. He's a perfect example of a monster who changes depending on his time. He began as, sort of, the A-bomb – this evil creature. Then he becomes a hero. Then he fought for the environment. Then he came back in the 80s as a terrible monster.

Godzilla is always changing – it's fabulous. He saves Japan, he destroys Japan. He's all-purpose. There are no bad Godzilla movies. Maybe the movie with the son of Godzilla wasn't that great, but my son loves it. The end of the movie where they freeze him – my son cried. Godzilla speaks a universal language. He speaks to all of us.

I'm Not Quite Feeling Myself Today…
Monstrous Mutations

Any type of monster is a mutation of sorts, but this motley gaggle of human and animal abominations demonstrates what damage can be done when nature makes a serious *faux pas*. On the surface, some of them may look like you and me, but dig a little deeper and you'll find that, no matter what their mutation, they're all freaks.

Freaks (1932)

Director: Tod Browning, USA

The written preamble for the movie *Freaks* could serve as a perfect introduction to this chapter on 'Monstrous Mutations'. Somewhat lengthy, but evocative in its establishment of what it means to be a 'blunder of nature' that is 'abnormal and unwanted', the scrolling card reads:

> 'In ancient times, anything that deviated from the normal was considered an omen of ill luck or representative of evil… History, religion, folklore and literature abound in tales of misshapen misfits who have altered the world's

course. Goliath, Calaban, Frankenstein, Gloucester, Tom Thumb and Kaiser Wilhelm are just a few whose fame is worldwide.'

What follows this introduction is one of cinema's bravest gestures, created by Tod Browning (*Dracula*, p.128) who had spent his early years living in a travelling circus. His goal was to expose the humanity beneath such socially unaccepted abnormalities – a testament to the old adage of 'beauty is only skin deep'.

Browning's means of communicating his message may have been a little too blatant, though, because, despite being a filmmaker of considerable repute, *Freaks* effectively ended his career. The film was banned in the UK for 30 years.

What was so abhorrent to the greater public was that Browning had utilised real 'freaks', rather than actors, in his film. Apparently, contrary to Browning's good intent, his performers were far too shocking for the average person to behold. Imagine the reaction to the film if Browning's original ending, where one of the film's able-bodied characters was castrated, had been included?

Regardless, *Freaks* has out-lived its controversy, surviving as both a deeply moralistic and important piece of early cinema and a work of morbid fascination. The tale is a simple one: a lovelorn midget is taken advantage of by a seductive trapeze artist who has her sights set on his inheritance. But there is nothing simple about *Freaks*.

This is a brazen, smart and moving film that should cement Tod Browning's reputation as an early master, even more than *Dracula*.

Physicality: The 'monsters' – as society would generally deem them – of *Freaks* appear in many different shapes, sizes, personalities and talents. For instance, there are the intriguing 'pinheads' of the film – scientifically termed 'microcephalics' – who appear abundantly enthusiastic and excitable; a couple of pint-sized 'doll people', who act as hinges at the dramatic centre of the plot; a bearded woman, a half-man/half-woman, conjoined twins and even a stuttering guy(!).

These curious sideshow people display even more intriguing qualities in their melding to an able-bodied world: a limbless man can still feed his nicotine habit by lighting a cigarette unassisted using only his mouth. An armless woman sips her beer elegantly by holding the stem of the glass between her toes without spilling a drop. A young woman sighs with ecstasy while experiencing the shared sensation of a lover's kiss enjoyed by her twin.

However, the duality of Browning's work means that, while society would consider these people as monsters, that is not the case in this film. The real monsters in *Freaks* are the two 'normal' people – society's ideal – whose intrinsic cruelty and sadism subjects the freaks to ridicule and, ultimately, leads to a plot of murder.

Personality: When embraced by others, the carnival freaks are warm, kind-hearted and good-humoured people. Yet they are largely viewed with suspicion by an uncaring world and, therefore, protect themselves with a guarded code of ethics.

At the wedding of one of the freaks with a supposedly normal person, the freaks express their acceptance of the unlikely union by chanting 'we accept her, we accept her, one of us, one of us' in a particularly chilling moment. Unnerved and possibly buckling under a guilty conscience, the evil bride resolutely proves she is undeserving of their admiration.

Lineage and Legacy: From *The Simpsons* to The Ramones, the 'one of us' chant from *Freaks* has been used again and again and again in popular culture, which gives some indication of the incredible influence of this film.

Whether Tod Browning regretted making this movie or not, the legacy of *Freaks* has lasted way beyond his own career and even his life. It has not been remade or sequelised, as doing so would be (almost) impossible – and, for that, we should all be extremely grateful.

It's Alive (1974)

Director: Larry Cohen, USA

Many people will refer to *It's Alive* as a B-movie, but somehow this label doesn't really fit properly. It's the early 70s so the cast is wearing flares and mutton chops. And, sure, the film is about a mutant baby that devours everything in its path, so it is decidedly 'B' in its premise. Somehow, though, auteur Larry Cohen's work rises above such pulpiness to an enviable level of sophistication.

As is constant across the majority of Cohen's films, *It's Alive* is well written, well acted and well executed, as well as being a sharp commentary on the divide between parents and their children in 1970s America. There is also a whole lot of subtext about abortion, genetic science and the like thrown into the melting pot.

Most storytellers would choose to flesh out the

mother/child relationship, but Cohen's spin concentrates on the push–pull of the father, brilliantly played by John P. Ryan. Does he destroy his own child or protect it? The anxiety heightens throughout the film as Ryan's character moves from one extreme to another. At one stage, he even wrestles with his own identity issues.

He says: 'When I was a kid, I used to think the monster was Frankenstein… you know, Karloff walking around in his big shoes grunting. I thought he was Frankenstein. Then I went to high school and read the book and I realised that Frankenstein was the doctor who created him. Somehow the identities get all mixed up, don't they?'

Read between the lines and you'll take more from *It's Alive* than what's merely on the screen. It says a lot for independent American filmmaking of that time.

Physicality: Six-time Academy Award winner Rick Baker was a young special-effects artist when he designed the baby for *It's Alive*, although Larry Cohen affords us only a few brief glimpses of his handiwork so as not to spoil the shock value.

As far as aggressive, mutated babies go, Baker set the standard – this monster sort of looks like a normal baby, except for the googly eyes, abnormal strength, sharp teeth and angry wail. Considering he's small (although a hefty size compared to the average human baby), he can hide in tight places, but he's also made of flesh and blood, which means he's not impervious to bullets and other physical attacks.

Personality: In the case of *It's Alive*, this baby is on a rampage the moment it breaks free from the birth canal – the delivery room resembling a slaughterhouse.

We're never sure why this abomination occurs. Hormone-fed chickens? Contaminated water supply? Overhead power lines? Whatever the reason, this baby is not content to lie in a crib and suckle at its mother's breast. However, in the presence of its family, it is as vulnerable as the next infant. All it needs it love.

Lineage and Legacy: In light of the success of *It's Alive*, Larry Cohen went on to make *It Lives Again* in 1978 and the straight-to-video *It's Alive III: Island of the Alive* in 1987. Cohen breaks his own rule in the first sequel and allows the babies to occupy far more screen time; however, the film is still highly effective – especially concerning 'goodies versus baddies' where the lines become cloudy.

It continues to live with a remake of the first film currently being completed.

Teeth (2006)

Director: Mitchell Lichtenstein, USA

Described by its filmmaker as 'a bit of a female revenge fantasy', *Teeth* presents a living embodiment of the *vagina dentata* – the beastly woman who overpowers men by chomping on their members with her jagged private parts – a myth that stretches back to tales first perpetuated in ancient times.

Over the years, horror stories (and movies) have pillaged from the *vagina dentata* legend in many different ways. Cinema theorists have debated its psychological meaning. Feminists have lambasted its subjugation of women. Film students have bandied it around as colourful dinner-party conversation.

In *Teeth*, first-time writer-director Mitchell Lichtenstein places the myth in a contemporary suburban context (or suburban hell), where teenagers live in their parents' garages, the streets are not tree lined or white picket fenced, and young people very rarely save their virginity until marriage. Dawn thinks otherwise, though, having taken an oath of chastity, and becomes her town's spokesperson on the subject. Her t-shirt reads 'Warning: sex changes everything' – and, as the story goes, sex with Dawn most certainly does.

Littered with sexual innuendo and symbolism – from vaginal knots in trees to phalluses in every scene – *Teeth* is simultaneously hilarious and horrifying in a way that cuts to the core of our most carnal selves. It is also full of noteworthy one-liners in a script that plays for laughs, possibly to undermine its unashamed goriness, like the classic 'reassurance' from Dawn's gynaecologist – 'Don't worry, I don't bite.'

Physicality: She is the girl-next-door – pretty, blonde and not as she seems. Lichtenstein is never so vulgar as to show us Dawn's *dentata* but, considering the damage it inflicts (and that damage will have all males in the audience grabbing at their crotches), it's a razor-sharp weapon that doesn't nibble, but bites clear through the flesh. Ouch.

Personality: While she preaches abstinence, Dawn manages to avoid being cloying and syrupy. She is smart, charismatic and passionately committed to her cause, which makes her a sought-after front-woman for the local chastity organisation and a prized sexual target for libidinous young men.

The charged performance by Jess Weixler as Dawn earned her a Special Jury Prize at the 2007 Sundance Film Festival and positions her as a talented young actress whose star deserves to be on the rise.

Lineage and Legacy: Dawn comes at the end of a long line of female monsters. She is the culmination of generations of misogyny that reaches back to the days when 'witches' were burnt at the stake. She is also indicative of horror cinema's move towards self-commentary, as prominently demonstrated in the satirical *Scary Movie* franchise.

How Dawn will affect cinema from this point onwards remains to be seen. But one thing is for sure: she is something both men and women are unlikely to forget quickly.

The Brood (1979)

Director: David Cronenberg, Canada

Filmmaker David Cronenberg acknowledges *The Brood* as his personal *Kramer vs. Kramer*, written following his own divorce and an ensuing custody battle. Considered in this context, the film is a sub-textual layer cake, spiced with all manner of psycho/sexual ingredients – gender politics, anger incarnations, evolution of the flesh… you name it, it's all there. For the theory-hungry student of psychology and/or philosophy, *The Brood* is a feast to be heartily devoured.

Adhering to Cronenberg's fascination with the (more often than not) grotesque physical manifestations of emotional states (*The Fly*, p.48; *Shivers*, p.131), *The Brood* sees two people in an uncomfortable marriage tousle, their only daughter caught like the meat in their sandwich. While the young girl lives with her father (Art Hindle), her mother

(Samantha Eggar) undergoes experimental treatment in the form of 'Psychoplasmics' – a controversial process whereby pent-up emotions are unleashed – behind the walls of a secluded 'institute' run by Dr Raglan (Oliver Reed).

As Dr Raglan's pet subject, the mother sinks deeply into the cushion of her treatment. However, even though she may be caged under lock and key, a number of mysterious attacks occur on people involved in her immediate family circle.

A scoot around the Internet will disclose much of the plotline of *The Brood*, although, for those yet to discover this fantastic film – the first of Cronenberg's more mature career phase – it would be best to just watch it before reading any in-depth analysis so as not to ruin the impact of a truly mind-blowing finale. If ever there was a proponent for 'taking a chill pill', *The Brood* is that movie.

Physicality: Without giving away too much, there are a couple of different monsters presented in this film. For argument's sake, though, we'll concentrate on the vengeful minions carrying out the killings.

These monsters are small. In fact, they are of a very similar height and build to the couple's young daughter. Clothed in red jackets with wispy blond hair framing their faces, they are also very much like this little girl in appearance – except, take a good look and they bear an uncanny facial resemblance to Oliver Reed. (Who knows whether this was intentional or not – it's just a personal observation.)

While they may be small in stature, they're speedy on their feet and deceptively strong. Just watch when one of them, armed with a paperweight, pummels a man to death with not one or two, but a succession of lethal blows.

Personality: There is little colour to the personality of these creatures – either they're completely docile, waiting for the next attack, or motivated by a frenzied rage. Anger is their sole motivation. They are tiny killing machines.

Lineage and Legacy: Even though the conclusion of *The Brood* leaves it open to a sequel, the film has never been sullied by follow-up. It is also one of those little gems – a 'wow' discovery – that you're likely to find in the discount bin at your local DVD outlet.

Given that *The Brood* is an important film in the Cronenberg oeuvre (note: it was the first movie on which composer Howard Shore collaborated with Cronenberg), it's a must-see for those who like their horror loaded with intelligence and meaning or those that are as suspicious of females as Cronenberg seems to be.

Cat People (1942)

Director: Jacques Tourneur, USA

Jacques Tourneur (*Night of the Demon*, p.68) may wear the director's hat here, but *Cat People* is universally known as a Val Lewton film – the creative producer whose indelible stamp defined every one of his noir-esque works.

Lewton came to make this moody piece when the RKO studio, reeling from the financial failures of Orson Welles' *Citizen Kane* and *The Magnificent Ambersons*, decided to muscle in on the horror/monster craze that was proving so popular over at Universal. He only had a micro budget of US$140,000 to play with, together with cast-off pieces of set from the higher-budget Welles movies, but couple that with an unbridled creativity that brought gothic horror into smalltown America, and Lewton created a cult classic that delivered a US$4 million return in box office for RKO.

Ironically, Lewton disliked cats, which may account for the deep sense of menace that infiltrates every frame of *Cat People*. Truly hypnotic and frightening, the film is high on suggestion and very low in graphic violence. It has been recognised as pioneering a trend in horror movies where tension rises in a supposed victim-and-prey stalking scene, only to dissipate into nothing (watch for the 'bus' sequence as an example).

Lewton's 'cat person' is the very sweet and kitten-like Simone Simon, an attractive French actress who plays the exotic Serbian Irena in *Cat People*, a loner hesitant to fall in love. Irena believes the women in her hometown can be traced back to a cursed race from Ancient Egypt who turn into cats when their passions are aroused.

Of course, this theory is dismissed as hogwash by her seducer, an all-American hero called Oliver Reed (the film was released when the actual Oliver Reed was four years old) played by Kent Smith. However, when Irena refuses to submit to him – even within the sanctuary of marriage – his frustrations see him turn to another woman. With anger coursing through her veins, the panther in Irena is unleashed, although to the audience it appears only as the darkening of her face and some wild animal noises.

Sexual repression, domestic anxieties and marital issues litter *Cat People*. It's powerful without ever spilling any blood.

Physicality: Considering Irena spends a lot of time lingering around the panther enclosure at a local zoo, we can only assume her monster form looks something like this sleek, black creature.

That's the thing about identifying the monster in *Cat People*; Lewton doesn't offer us even a glimpse of a transformed Irena. In fact, could the cat manifestation simply be a figment of her imagination? That's a question we, and some of the characters, continue to ask from the start through to the finish of the film. Whatever the answer, sweet Irena is very good at scaring people.

Personality: Seemingly the damsel in distress, Irena looks like she wouldn't hurt a fly. She speaks with a delicate accented voice and fits snugly into Ollie's embrace whenever she's in need of comfort.

Her husband starts as her perfect match – possessing the patience of a saint – who is willing to help his lovely wife through her strange neuroses and desist from pressuring her into fulfilling his physical desires. It is only when another woman steps onto the scene that Irena's sweet voice drips with venom and her eyes take on a steely veneer.

Lineage and Legacy: Val Lewton followed up *Cat People* with a sequel called *The Curse of the Cat People* (1944), which was directed by Gunther von Fritsch and Robert Wise, following up themes from the first movie, but strangely lacking a monster.

A contemporary audience will be most familiar with the Paul Schrader version of the original film released in 1982, which starred Nastassja Kinski and Malcolm McDowell.

Enjoyable in its own right, the Schrader film, not surprisingly, ups the sensuality/sexuality of the Lewton film; however, the storyline is only a loose adaptation. A respectable homage, nonetheless.

And Then Some...

Attack of the 50 Foot Woman (1958)

Director: Nathan Juran, USA

As a straight-up exercise in camp, *Attack of the 50 Foot Woman* retains a sense of cool, even 50 years after its cinema release. Its title alone is something that intrigues. Couple that with its poster art – a large-scale Allison Hayes looming over a highway wielding a car in her hand – and you've got an iconic t-shirt design that continues to magnetise teenagers who've possibly never seen the film.

That's not to say that this is a good movie (although it's certainly better than the 1993 remake starring Daryl Hannah). It's pretty bad in terms of filmmaking aesthetics, but completely loveable. When it comes to cornball, 50s, large-mutated-monster movies, *Attack of the 50 Foot Woman* is the cookie cutter all others have sought to emulate.

Taking its inspiration from other human-size-altering movies like *The Amazing Colossal Man*, the plot is kind of a revenge-of-the-disgruntled-housewife film. Saddled with a philandering husband and a drinking problem, no one believes Nancy Archer when she finds an alien spacecraft in the desert. But then, after she grows to a height of 50 foot following radiation exposure, people start to see her in a different light.

OK – yes – she is a big monster, but considering she is also a human being, Nancy gets to reside under the 'Monstrous Mutations' category.

Eraserhead (1976)

Director: David Lynch, USA

Some may argue that *Eraserhead* is not a monster movie because, basically, it is just the kind of film that people argue about. Disturbing, even though the film's non-linear story-line makes it difficult to decipher what is actually happening, it unfurls with the confusion, mood and abstraction of a dark dream – at a guess, *Eraserhead* is like probing the inside of David Lynch's brain.

The monster in question is the mutant infant that Jack Nance's aggravated girlfriend brings into the world. Wrapped tightly in bandages, this baby whines constantly, and appears to have nothing but a stump as a body, along with a non-human head comprising snout-like nose and eyes positioned on either side of its head. It was rumoured that this creature was created from the embalmed foetus of a calf. Not attractive at all.

Whatever the interpretation of *Eraserhead*, Lynch has said that no interpretation agrees with his own. This is a film to be experienced rather than understood, but also one that has a monster that would test any expectant parents' levels of anxiety.

Basket Case (1982)

Director: Frank Henenlotter, USA

Seedy, cheap and gore-sodden, *Basket Case* is one of those movies that puts the 'low' in low budget. Apparently, while filming some of the scenes, even the crew walked off the set offended, which says a lot for Frank Henenlotter's debut as a filmmaker.

The story sees a young man arrive in New York City carrying his abominably deformed conjoined twin in a basket – and when we say 'abominably deformed', the twin is nothing more than a living blob of flesh with a bad temper and a high sex drive. The two seemingly inseparable siblings are on a mission: to murder the three doctors who turned them into two people after so many years of being one and the same.

Basket Case isn't going to be everyone's idea of a night's entertainment, but regardless of its technical shoddiness and blatant shock value, it has lingered at the back of video stores in the cult-classic section. The rental market loved it; Henenlotter even went on to make two further sequels... and let's not forget the super-duper-fun *Brain Damage* (1988) about a jolly blue phallic worm that feasts on people's brains.

From the Desk of...
Larry Cohen
(USA)

'The Host *obviously brings to mind* Godzilla, *but Bong says his inspiration was Larry Cohen's* Q: The Winged Serpent, *a 1982 film in which a creature swoops down from its nest on the Chrysler Building to attack unlucky New Yorkers.'* – review of *The Host* by V.A. Musetto, *New York Post* (9 March 2007)

Filmography: *It's Alive* (1974), *God Told Me To* (1976), *It Lives Again* (1978), *Q – The Winged Serpent* (1982), *It's Alive III: Island of the Alive* (1987)

Monsters have been in everything from our childhoods. All the little fairytales and folk stories that we heard had monsters in them. There's *Jack and the Beanstalk* with the giant, the witch in *Hansel and Gretel* who baked the children in the oven, *Snow White and the Seven Dwarfs* with the vicious queen... They all have elements of power and fear in there... and kids love it.

My kids would always say to me at bedtime, 'Dad, tell us a spooky story,' and I'd make something up for them. If it makes them feel scared, then they feel safe because they're in their parents' arms. So the same thing applies to the movies.

People go to the movies and get scared, but they're secure in the fact that it's only a movie. They're not really in any danger.

Girls love it because they get to cuddle up to their boyfriends and act feminine and afraid, and the boyfriend gets to be protective, put his arms around her, and cop a feel – so he's enjoying himself. Everybody likes horror movies and it will be like that forever. There are good ones and there are bad ones. You get enough bad ones and it kills the cycle for a while because people get sick of seeing bad movies. But then a good one comes along and the whole cycle starts again.

There are certain people who profess they don't like horror movies because they're too childish or too excessive, but then they'll give an Academy Award to *The Silence of the Lambs* that has a cannibal running around biting people on the face. It all depends on how well it's done. If it's done well like *Alien* or *The Exorcist*, then it crosses all the barriers and it reaches everyone.

The best monster movies in my thinking are the ones where you see the least of the monster. You keep waiting to get a look at it – it's there but you never *really* get a good look. You only get to see sections of the monster in the first *Alien* movie. In *Jaws*, you waited for over an hour before you got to see the monster for the first time – it was down below the surface, but you didn't see it.

I tried to do the same with *It's Alive*, which was made before *Jaws*. You saw very little of the monster and you kept wanting to see more. You didn't get to see enough of it to have a full understanding of how it really looked, so you were still afraid of it.

No matter how good the monster is, if you put it on the screen long enough, people get used to it and then it ceases to be frightening. It just becomes interesting. They might say how well it was effected, or how great the animation was, or how good the prosthetics were, but it's not scary any more. The audience might become enamoured with the technique, but they're not afraid any more. We always fear what we can't see – what's hiding in the dark.

Many of my films that I've written I've also directed, so when I want the monster to appear in the film, I draw a rendering of what I think the monster's going to look like and then I give it to the special-effects people and they go from there. Not everybody does that, but I always like to play a part in the whole process.

Many films are made by different departments, where the special-effects people, more or less, take over the movie – it's their movie. The film then has the look – the stamp – of whatever company has done the special effects. Whether it's Stan Winston's company or ILM… all those pictures have a similar look to them.

I made Q – *The Winged Serpent* after I was fired from *I, the Jury*. I didn't get along with the producers. They were just under-financed and terrible people. I didn't want the people who were kind enough to give me equipment and who had faith in me to get screwed, so I told these people that the company didn't have enough money to pay the bills. The producers heard what I'd said to everybody and then they fired me. But it all worked out OK in the end because, if they hadn't fired me from *I, the Jury*, then I wouldn't have made Q.

The day after being fired, I decided to stay in New York

and make Q, so I started shooting the very next day. I got a crew together and we did the helicopter stuff. That was pretty scary, flying in-between the spires of all those build-ings. I remember we flew right up to the twin towers too – just a little left without going through them. It looks like we go through the gap because we zoomed in when we got close enough to the space between the two towers. Now that I realise those buildings are gone, I feel quite sad.

By the end of the week, we had the actors and we were shooting and making a movie. The other people from *I, the Jury* couldn't believe we were making Q. We finished shooting before them and we opened in theatres in New York on the same day. Q did three times the box office of *I, the Jury* – total vindication. The company that made *I, the Jury* also went into bankruptcy and that was the end of them.

Q was a pretty complicated movie to make with special effects and everything. But I just did it. I knew where every-thing was supposed to go. I decided to shoot it my way and then the special-effects people just had to do what I wanted them to do.

One of the guys who did the special effects – Randy Cook – he just worked on Jackson's *King Kong*. He actually played the pilot in the plane that shoots King Kong at the end of the film. Well, Randy was flabbergasted with my approach – 'You don't do it this way – you work it out with us and we tell you where to put all the monster stuff.' I said, 'Well, it's too late now. Do the best you can.' They told me it wouldn't work because the camera was moving when the monster was moving. Having the helicopter footage swooping around the Chrysler Building wouldn't work because the camera was always in motion. I said, 'You'll make it work – you'll put the bird in motion too.' The special-effects guys weren't too happy about it.

Nobody quite knew what that Quetzalcoatl big bird god looked like, except for some very crude drawings, so the special-effects makers – David Allen and Randy Cook – designed the monster in their imagination. I think they made the thing a little too heavy. It should have been sleeker and a little lighter in form. That damn thing didn't look like it could get off the ground very well. But frankly, they were putting up with me and my odd way of making a special-effects picture, so I went along with them. Although I wish today that I'd been a little more demanding on the design of the monster.

I thought the Chrysler Building was a prettier building than the Empire State Building in *King Kong*. I thought that the Chrysler Building deserved its own monster. It had all these bird images on it – a feathered design and birds sculpted into the sides... really beautiful. I thought, if a bird was ever going to find a place to nest, it would certainly pick the sparkly, glittery dome of the Chrysler Building.

We couldn't afford to build the Chrysler Building, so we shot it up there at the very top of the building, 86 storeys above the street. We had to hoist all the cameras, all the equipment up there. All the actors had to climb little ladders to get up there. We even had to get pigeon wranglers to take up pigeons.

It was a big, empty spire with no barricades to keep you from falling off. You just stepped right off the building – like being on a platform 86 storeys above the streets of New York. I had a stuntman following me around holding on to my belt from the back, just to make sure I didn't fall. If I had fallen off the building, it would have made the people on *I, the Jury* very happy.

When they made the *Godzilla* remake – the big-budget one by Roland Emmerich – they basically took the story from *Q*. You realise, in the other Godzilla movies, Godzilla wasn't female? Godzilla was not laying eggs. Suddenly, Godzilla was laying eggs in Manhattan. In my movie, it was the Chrysler Building. In their movie, it was Madison Square Garden. The way I shot *Q* and the way they shot *Godzilla* are identical too. When they discover there's a new egg that's been left behind, it's shot in exactly the same way – the egg cracks open and the titles come up. That's exactly from *Q*.

I didn't know *It's Alive* was going to be as successful as it was. It was number one at the box office in America for a few weeks, and overseas it was very big. In fact, it was the second-biggest-grossing movie in Singapore in the history of Warner Bros Studios – out-grossed by *My Fair Lady*. Well, I thought that was really funny. I'm glad it did so well over there, but it didn't mean a thing to the Warner Bros people in Hollywood until the picture opened in America and did business there too.

Back in the 70s when we made the picture, there were so many people alienated from their children – kids who were growing up to be teenagers, taking drugs, growing their hair long, dressing in objectionable ways, engaging in blatant sexual activity. Many middle-class American families felt like they had a stranger living in their house. Their adorable little child had grown up to be this unpleasant individual who was so defiant and angry and so aggressive and so doped up.

There were several cases where fathers actually killed their children – shot their teenagers. I'd read about it in the newspapers. My God – what it must be like to want to kill your own child because he's become a monster. And I thought, 'Oh, that's an interesting idea.' Suppose a monster is born into an ordinary American family – how do they reconcile their love for this infant and the fact that it's an abnormal creature bringing death and destruction to other people?

Of course, anybody who has a son who's a criminal or murderer faces this kind of quandary – how can they love their child when their child has gone out and killed three or four people? It happens all the time. Everybody who is a murderer has parents. Everybody that's a murderer was a child once.

If you look at the formula for *It's Alive*, it bears a mirror image to *E.T.* In *E.T.*, these people bring a benevolent monster into their home and hide it while the police and the government are trying to locate the creature and kill it. In *It's Alive*, they bring an abnormal creature into their house, which is their child, and hide it from the authorities, even though it kills – probably in its own defence. Spielberg, I'm sure, saw the *It's Alive* picture and subconsciously absorbed it. There are a lot of images from *It's Alive* that turned up in *E.T.* too. The opening of *It's Alive* with the flashlights – the opening of *E.T.* has the flashlights in the woods. If you look at both pictures, you'll see the similarities.

It's Alive was a scary idea. And people hadn't seen that movie before. They'd seen *Rosemary's Baby*, which was about the birth of the Devil, but that picture ends with the birth. It more or less ends where *It's Alive* begins, although I can tell you that *It's Alive* wasn't influenced by *Rosemary's Baby*, even though a lot of people have compared the two. If we'd made *It's Alive* about the mother, then it would have been too much like *Rosemary's Baby*, whereas doing it from the father's point of view makes it different.

There's been a remake of *It's Alive*. It's been shot over in Europe... and it's terrible. Awful. I don't make any bones about it either. I mean, I took their money, so they have rights, and I let them do it, but, I must say, they made a shambles of it. That's OK, though – people will think my version is *Gone with the Wind*. I wouldn't recommend it to any of my fans. I'd tell them to cross the street. It's unwatchable.

In the old days of monster sci-fi movies in the 50s and 60s, the characters were always very cardboard – dull. Usually, there was some pretty girl with big breasts onscreen saying how she was a physicist or something totally ridiculous like that. The actors they hired were dull. They all had that square, heroic look to them.

Once in a while, you got a good movie like *Them!*, for example. There were some interesting characters in that one. My approach to monster movies was to make these pictures as real stories with real people. *Creature from the Black Lagoon* was a pretty good little movie. I liked that one. But still, there had to be a pretty girl so that the monster could pull her off the deck and swim away with her.

From when I was a child, I remember the original *Thing* very well and I remember *Them!*, which I saw the first day at the Paramount Theatre in New York – I was the first one to buy a ticket. Of course, I loved the Karloff Frankenstein movies. I thought his performance was so remarkable, particularly in the *Bride of Frankenstein*. Those pictures had a big effect on me. It's always the ones you see as a child that have the greatest impact on you.

Index

190

INDEX